# THE FARM GARDEN

THE CLASSIC USDA FARMERS' BULLETIN NO. 1673
WITH TIPS AND TRADITIONAL METHODS
IN SUSTAINABLE GARDENING AND PERMACULTURE

### BY U.S. DEPARTMENT OF AGRICULTURE

ORIGINALLY PUBLISHED IN 1931

## LEGACY EDITION
CLASSIC FARMERS BULLETIN LIBRARY
BOOK NO. 1673

**Doublebit Press**
Eugene, OR

*New content, introduction, and annotations*
*Copyright © 2020 by Doublebit Press. All rights reserved.*

*Doublebit Press is an imprint of Eagle Nest Press*
*www.doublebitpress.com | Eugene, OR, USA*

*Original content under the public domain. Originally published in 1931 by the U.S. Department of Agriculture.*

*This title, along with other Doublebit Press books including the Classic Farmers Bulletin Library, are available at a volume discount for youth groups, outdoors clubs, or reading groups.*

*Doublebit Press Legacy Edition ISBN*
*Paperback: 978-1-64389-130-9*

*Disclaimer: Because of its age and historic context, this book could contain content on present-day inappropriate methods, activities, outdated medical information, unsafe chemical and mechanical processes, or culturally and racially insensitive content. Doublebit Press, or its employees, authors, and other affiliates, assume no liability for any actions performed by readers or any damages that might be related to information contained in this book. This text has been published for historical study and for personal literary enrichment toward the goal of preserving the American handcraft tradition, timeless trade skills, and traditional artisanal knowledge.*

*First Doublebit Press Legacy Edition Printing, 2020*

*Printed in the United States of America when purchased at retail in the USA*

# Introduction
## Classic Farmers Bulletin Library

The old experts of artisanal trades, country and homestead knowledge, and the woods and mountains taught timeless principles and skills for centuries. Through their timeless books, the old experts offered rich descriptions of how the world works and encouraged learning through personal experiences *by doing*. Over the last 125 years, manufacturing, farming, and construction have substantially changed. Of course, many things have gotten simpler as equipment and technology have improved. In addition, some activities of pre-digital times are now no longer in vogue, or are even outright considered inappropriate or illegal. However, despite many of the positive changes in manufacturing and crafting methods that have occurred over the years, *there are many other skills and much knowledge that have been forgotten.*

By publishing the reprint series of the old USDA *Farmers' Bulletin*, it is our goal at Doublebit Press to do what we can to preserve and share the works from forgotten teachers that form the cornerstone of the history of the American artisans and traditional crafts. So much farm, homestead, and handcraft knowledge was passed to each generation through experience and hard work. An original mission of the US Department of Agriculture was to optimize farm outputs and increase the quality of life on farms through handcrafts, construction, and old-time farm tricks, tips, and skills. In their *Farmers' Bulletin* series, the USDA captured and passed on knowledge that applied to far more than just farmers!

Through remastered reprint editions of timeless classics, perhaps we can regain some of this lost knowledge for future generations. Today's interest in mastery of old handcraft skills, homestead self-sufficiency, and artisanal character has renewed an interest in the old arts. Luckily, the USDA's *Farmers' Bulletin* series contains thousands of pamphlets dedicated to teaching, improving life, and ensuring self-sufficiency to thrive in both the city and on a farm.

This book is an important contribution traditional handcraft and country skills literature and has important historical and collector value toward preserving the American handcraft and outdoors tradition. The knowledge it holds is an invaluable reference for practicing skills and hand craft methods. Its chapters thoroughly discuss some of the essential building blocks of knowledge that are fundamental but may have been forgotten as equipment gets fancier and technology gets smarter. In short, this reprint of the *Farmers' Bulletin* pamphlets was chosen for Legacy Edition printing because much of the basic skills and knowledge it contains has been forgotten or put to the wayside in trade for more modern conveniences and methods.

With technology playing a major role in everyday life, sometimes we need to take a step back in time to find those basic building blocks used for gaining mastery – the things that we have luckily not completely lost and has been recorded in books over the last two centuries. These skills aren't forgotten, they've just been shelved. *It's time to unshelve them once again and reclaim the lost knowledge of self-sufficiency.*

Based on this commitment to preserving our outdoors and handcraft artisanal heritage, we have taken great pride in publishing this book as a complete original work. We hope it is worthy of both study and collection by outdoors folk in the modern era of outdoors and traditional skills life.

Unlike many other photocopy reproductions of classic books that are common on the market, this Legacy Edition does not simply place poor photography of old texts on our pages and use error-prone optical scanning or computer-generated text. We want our work to speak for itself, and reflect the quality demanded by our customers who spend their hard-earned money. With this in mind, each Legacy Edition book that has been chosen for publication is carefully remastered from original print books, *with the Doublebit Legacy Edition printed and laid out in the exact way that it was presented at its original publication.* We provide a beautiful, memorable experience that is as true to the original text as best as possible, but with the aid of modern technology to make as beautiful a reading experience as possible for books that can be over a century old.

Because of its age and because it is presented in its original form, the book may contain misspellings, inking errors from print plates, and other printing blemishes that were common for the age. However, these are exactly the things that we feel give the book its character, which we preserved in this Legacy Edition. During digitization, we ensured that each illustration in the text was clean and sharp with the least amount of loss from being copied and digitized as possible. Full-page plate illustrations are presented as they were found, often including the extra blank page that was often behind a plate. For the covers, we use the original cover design to give the book its original feel. We are sure you'll appreciate the fine touches and attention to detail that your Legacy Edition has to offer.

For traditional handcrafters and classic artisanal enthusiasts who demand the best from their equipment, this Doublebit Press Legacy Edition reprint was made with you in mind. Both important and minor details have equally both been accounted for by our publishing staff, down to the cover, font, layout, and images. It is the goal of Doublebit Legacy Edition series to be worthy of collection in any outdoorsperson's library and that can be passed to future generations.

Every book selected to be in this series offers unique views and instruction on important skills, advice, tips, tidbits, anecdotes, stories, and experiences that will enrich the repertoire of any person who enjoys escaping a bit from today's modern technology-based, cookie-cutter, and highly industrialized skills. Instead, folks seeking to make things with their hands like the old days may find great value from these resurrected instructional manuals from the past. These books were not simply written to be shelved in a library – they contain our history and forgotten methods to make things with real character and energy with a *human* component.

Therefore, to learn the most basic building blocks of a craft leads to mastery of all its aspects. We hope this book helps you along this path with its rich descriptions and illustrations!

**About the USDA Farmers' Bulletin Series**

Back in the early 1900s, the US Department of Agriculture (USDA) began publication of small pamphlets that were meant to improve the outputs of America's farms, promote self-sufficiency, and help farmers and farming communities thrive. This publication series continued for decades, and volumes were always available when someone wanted to learn more about a specific skill or topic that could come in handy on the homestead.

Each of the 2,000+ volumes specializes in one specific topic, be it growing a certain crop, raising a particular animal, or building a type of farm structure. Each of the pamphlets captured the best knowledge available at that time, which often represented decades or centuries of old farmer knowledge, which we know, is incredibly useful and reliable!

As we continue to blaze paths into the digital frontier, many of these lost "farmers' tips" have become more useful than ever, particularly to folks looking to start homesteads and small-scale farms, as well as those who just want to live more sustainably, simply, and consciously in light of today's factory processed world. The *Farmers' Bulletin* is also highly useful for people who live in cities, as they contain much information for community gardens, urban and rooftop farming, and sustainable living tips.

Unfortunately, many of these print volumes of the *Farmers' Bulletin* are now out of print. Indeed, because these texts are in the public domain, they are easily found and are available on the Internet. However, many of these books that are easily found on the web are often low-resolution photocopies, complete with scribble marks or other distracting spots. For the first time, high-quality, professionally restored *Farmers' Bulletin* reissues are being made by Doublebit Press to increase access to the timeless knowledge that each contains.

This Doublebit Press Legacy Edition republishes this tradition of handcrafted quality and artisanal work. We hope that this deluxe printed edition of this book will help you gain mastery in your craft, as it is presented in the exact form that it was originally published. Even today, the knowledge contained within its pages are timeless and have much to teach!

Finally, as works of art, the USDA *Farmers' Bulletin* issues contain beautiful illustrations and line art that are a sign of simpler, yet authentic times when quality mattered and craftsmanship was king. This collectible volume makes a great addition to the bookshelf of any handcrafter, maker, artisan, farmer, homesteader, or outdoors enthusiast!

Enjoy some old-time, vintage charm when the government actually encouraged you to be self-sufficient with these beautifully illustrated and classic instruction manuals by the USDA!

# U.S. DEPARTMENT OF AGRICULTURE
## FARMERS' BULLETIN No. 1673

# The FARM GARDEN

FARM GARDENS, maintained on about four-fifths of the farms in the United States as a source of wholesome family food supply, are annually saving millions of dollars for the farmers of the country. A well-cared-for garden will yield a greater return per acre than any similar area on the farm devoted to regular farm crops.

A good garden adds very materially to the well-being of the farm family by supplying foods that might not otherwise be provided. Fresh vegetables direct from the garden are superior in quality to those generally sold on the market, and in addition are readily available when wanted for use.

Certain crops may be grown in southern gardens throughout the winter; in fact, there are thousands of southern farm gardens that produce at least one or two fresh vegetables every day in the year. The northern gardening season may be greatly extended by the use of hotbeds and coldframes, also by planting the more hardy late-summer and fall crops.

This bulletin supersedes Farmers' Bulletins 934, Home Gardening in the South, and 937, The Farm Garden in the North.

## INDEX OF VEGETABLES

| Vegetable | Page | Vegetable | Page |
|---|---|---|---|
| Artichoke, Jerusalem | 43 | Kohlrabi | 59 |
| Asparagus | 28 | Leek | 60 |
| Beans | 52 | Lettuce | 30 |
| Beet | 41 | Martynia | 66 |
| Broccoli, heading | 55 | Muskmelon | 50 |
| Broccoli, sprouting | 55 | Mustard | 34 |
| Brussels sprouts | 55 | Okra | 66 |
| Cabbage | 56 | Onion | 61 |
| Cabbage, Chinese | 57 | Parsley | 40 |
| Cardoon | 31 | Parsley, turnip-rooted | 48 |
| Carrot | 42 | Parsnip | 44 |
| Cauliflower | 58 | Peas | 54 |
| Celeriac | 43 | Peppers | 63 |
| Celery | 36 | Physalis | 66 |
| Chard | 32 | Poke | 30 |
| Chervil | 43 | Potato | 44 |
| Chicory, witloof | 38 | Pumpkin | 50 |
| Chives | 59 | Radish | 45 |
| Collards | 59 | Rhubarb | 30 |
| Corn salad | 38 | Rutabaga | 47 |
| Corn, sweet | 66 | Salsify | 46 |
| Cress, upland | 40 | Shallot | 62 |
| Cress, water | 41 | Sorrel | 36 |
| Cucumber | 49 | Spinach | 34 |
| Dandelion | 33 | Spinach, New Zealand | 35 |
| Dasheen | 43 | Squash | 51 |
| Eggplant | 63 | Sweetpotato | 46 |
| Endive | 33 | Tomato | 64 |
| Fennel, Florence | 65 | Turnip | 47 |
| Garlic | 60 | Turnip greens | 36 |
| Horseradish | 29 | Watermelon | 51 |
| Kale | 33 | | |

Washington, D. C.      Issued October, 1931

# THE FARM GARDEN

By J. H. BEATTIE, *Associate Horticulturist*, and W. R. BEATTIE, *Senior Horticulturist, Division of Horticultural Crops and Diseases, Bureau of Plant Industry*

## CONTENTS

| | Page | | Page |
|---|---|---|---|
| General information | 1 | General information—Continued. | 25 |
| Value of the farm garden | 1 | Irrigation | 25 |
| Soil and location | 1 | Paper mulch | 26 |
| Protecting the garden | 2 | Insects and diseases | 27 |
| Fertilizers | 3 | Canning and storing vegetables at home | 27 |
| Lime | 5 | Culture of specific garden crops | 27 |
| Soil preparation | 6 | Perennial vegetables | 27 |
| Plan and arrangement | 6 | Greens | 31 |
| Seed supply | 8 | Salad crops | 36 |
| Starting early plants | 6 | Root and tuber-root crops | 41 |
| Southern-grown plants | 12 | Vine crops (cucurbits) | 48 |
| Transplanting | 12 | Legumes | 52 |
| Time of planting | 14 | Cabbage group | 54 |
| Planting the garden | 18 | Onion group | 59 |
| Succession of crops | 23 | Fleshy-fruited warm-season crops | 63 |
| The late summer and fall garden | 23 | Miscellaneous vegetables | 65 |
| Cultivation | 24 | | |

## GENERAL INFORMATION

### VALUE OF THE FARM GARDEN

FARM GARDENS are maintained on approximately 79 per cent of all farms in the United States, the average value of the products per garden being estimated at $68, or a total of about $350,000,000. A half-acre garden, if properly cared for, will supply vegetables having a market value of at least $100 to $150, sufficient for a family of five or six. The main arguments in favor of a good garden on the farm, however, are that the vegetables are available when needed, are fresh, and have high quality and flavor. These characteristics are not present to the same degree in vegetables bought on the markets, especially those shipped long distances or kept in storage and subjected to handling and exposure.

During busy periods on the farm it is not always possible to go to market for fresh vegetables, and the farm garden becomes a convenient time-saving source of supply. Recent discoveries as to the vitamin content of fresh vegetables, especially the leafy kinds, emphasize the value of the garden in safeguarding the family's health. Crops that require considerable space, such as sweet corn, potatoes, sweetpotatoes, winter squashes, and melons, generally may be grown to best advantage outside the garden and in connection with the cultivation of field crops, leaving the smaller crops to the garden proper.

### SOIL AND LOCATION

Good soil is the first essential for a successful garden. The type of soil is not so important as that it be well drained, well supplied with organic matter, retentive of moisture, easy to work, and reasonably free from weeds. Sandy loam soils usually can be worked earlier in the spring than the stiff clay loams, but crops on the clay loams frequently withstand dry weather better than those on the lighter soils. By means of drainage, irrigation, manuring, and the right type of cultivation any reasonably good soil can be made suitable for the intensive production of vegetables.

The slope of the land has considerable influence upon the time when the garden can be planted. A gentle slope toward the south or southeast is favorable for early crops. A location that is protected on the north by a hill, a group of close-growing trees, buildings, a stone wall, or a tight board fence is desirable in sections where winds are likely to cause damage to crops.

Hedges make good windbreaks, but owing to their heavy shade and draft on soil moisture and plant food they may prove undesirable in some locations. Arborvitae and California and Amur River privet are most commonly used for hedges around gardens, and if kept closely pruned they are in general fairly satisfactory. In place of a hedge, strips of burlap fastened to the garden fence or to lines of stakes around and through the garden give a fair protection against soil blowing and wind damage. Frequently irrigation is employed to prevent soil blowing and consequent injury to crops. Tightly constructed board fences make good windbreaks for gardens.

Good drainage is essential, and, if possible, the garden should be located on well-drained land. The drainage may often be improved by the addition of tile drains, open ditches, or the loosening of the soil by subsoiling. The garden should be free from depressions in which water might stand after a heavy rain. Waste water from surrounding land should not be allowed to drain upon the garden, and the fall below the garden should be such that there will be no danger of flood water backing up on it. The garden should not be located on creek or river-bottom land subject to overflow during the growing season.

The location of the garden for convenience both in caring for the crops and in gathering the vegetables is of great importance. It should be as near the dwelling as circumstances permit.

Sunlight is a vital factor in the production of vegetables, and for this reason the garden should be situated where it will receive the direct rays of the sun. Certain crops may stand more shading than others, but no amount of fertilizer, water, or care will replace sunshine. Trees not only shade the garden but draw heavily upon the moisture and fertility of the soil. Even where trees are so located that they do not shade the garden, their presence is a menace, for their roots may penetrate far into the garden and rob the crops of moisture and plant food.

### PROTECTING THE GARDEN

Under most conditions the garden should be surrounded by a fence sufficiently high and close-woven to keep out poultry, dogs, rabbits, and other animals. In certain sections wild deer frequently destroy gardens, in which case it may be necessary to surround the garden with a fence 8 to 12 feet high. In the Great Plains area jack rabbits are a menace to gardens, but they may be kept out by the use of a rabbit-tight fence. Where the common cottontail rabbit is troublesome, gardens may be protected by either a woven wire or a closely spaced picket fence.

Poultry, especially chickens, are the most common source of injury to farm gardens. Two methods of protection are open to the garden owner—fencing the garden or confining the poultry to a definite inclosure, whichever may be the more desirable or practical. In any event, if crops are to be grown, poultry must be kept out of the garden.

Rodents of various kinds are sources of trouble to garden crops in certain sections of the country. In the East, moles and two or three species of mice cause much injury. They can be controlled by trapping, poisoning, and the use of poisons or repellents placed in their runs. Temporary relief from these rodents can generally be obtained by injecting small quantities of carbon disulphide into their runs. The exhaust gas from an automobile has the same effect. Moth balls dropped into the runs may be effective in driving off moles, but can hardly be depended on as a certain protection. In the West where ground squirrels and prairie dogs are prevalent, poisoning is the usual and most effective remedy.[1]

### FERTILIZERS

Stable or barn-lot manure is the best garden fertilizer for use on most soils, except where the land is already oversupplied with organic matter, which is rarely the case. An initial application of 20 large wagonloads of partly rotted manure on a half-acre garden is not excessive. Following this, 8 to 10 tons of manure should be applied each year, unless there is evidence that the soil is becoming too rich in organic matter for certain crops like tomatoes and beans. After this stage is reached, the manure should be applied only to that portion of the garden on which crops that require heavy fertilizing are to be planted. The time of applying the manure will vary, but as a rule it should be spread just before plowing. Inasmuch as the garden is usually planted very shortly after plowing, it is desirable that the manure should be well rotted and rather fine. Coarse or strawy manure not only may interfere with the cultivation of the crops, but does not give as good results as does thoroughly rotted manure. Some farmers follow the practice of first plowing the garden, then spreading several loads of well-composted manure over the surface and working it into the soil with a disk harrow.

The addition of 50 to 80 pounds of superphosphate to each ton of manure, either in the stable or during the composting period, will aid in the decomposition of the manure and also greatly increase its value as a fertilizer. The usual method of composting manure is to place the required quantity in a low, flat pile and turn it once every week or 10 days until it has been turned three or four times. After the third or fourth turning the manure can be allowed to remain in a flat pile until wanted for spreading on the garden. If the manure is dry, water should be added to prevent burning.

---

[1] Full information on the poisoning of rodents can be procured from the Bureau of Biological Survey, U. S. Department of Agriculture.

Where large quantities of manure are being hauled from a feed lot to the fields, it is often possible to save a few loads of the finer material or scrapings for use on the garden.

Sheep and goat manures are extensively used in parts of the West and Southwest. On farms where large flocks of poultry are kept there is often a considerable accumulation of poultry manure, which may be used at a rate not exceeding 100 pounds for each 1,000 square feet. It should be borne in mind that sheep, goat, and poultry manures contain a high percentage of nitrogen and therefore should be used sparingly; otherwise injury to crops may occur. This is particularly true when commercial pulverized sheep manure is applied directly around growing plants, and great care must be taken to spread the manure thinly and mix it with the soil rather than to place it in direct contact with the plants. Where poultry, sheep, or goat manure is being used in making hills for cucumbers, melons, or squashes, it should be mixed with the soil to a depth of at least 6 inches over an area 18 to 24 inches in diameter.

### SPECIAL FERTILIZERS AND COMPOST

Every farm garden should be provided with a compost pile from which a supply of fine, rich soil for growing plants may be available at all times. The ideal method of making a compost pile is to stack sods or turf with an equal quantity of manure, let the pile rot, then mix and screen for use. It usually requires about a year for material of this kind to rot, and it may be necessary to add a little water from time to time to give it the right degree of moisture for proper decay. Spading or turning the compost heap occasionally will hasten the process of decay, but, as a rule, merely piling the materials together in a heap will give fair results. The manure from the hotbed, sods or rich soil that may be available, and the poultry-house floor cleanings all may go into the compost pile to form soil for use on the garden or for growing early plants. The refuse from garden crops should not go into the compost because of the danger of spreading plant diseases.

Sterilizing the soil used for starting early plants by baking it slowly in the oven for an hour or two not only will greatly reduce the danger of plant losses from soil-borne diseases but will also destroy many of the weed seeds that are present in the soil.

Commercial fertilizers may be used to advantage in many farm gardens, the composition and rate of application depending on the locality, soil, and crops to be grown. For general use, a fertilizer containing 5 per cent nitrogen, 10 per cent phosphoric acid, and 5 or 6 per cent potash will give good results. Leafy crops, such as spinach, cabbage, kale, and lettuce, often require a higher percentage of nitrogen and may be stimulated by side dressings of nitrate of soda or some other form of readily available nitrogen. As a rule the root crops, including beets, carrots, turnips, and parsnips, need a higher percentage of potash. A fertilizer for potatoes may contain as much as 8 or 10 per cent of potash in addition to nitrogen and phosphoric acid.

The quantity of fertilizer to use will depend upon the condition of the soil, its natural fertility, and the crops being grown. Tomatoes and beans, for example, do not normally require a great amount of fertilizer, especially nitrogen; whereas onions, celery, lettuce, the root crops, and potatoes will respond to relatively large applications. In some cases 300 pounds of commercial fertilizer may be sufficient on a half-acre garden;[2] in other cases 1,000 or 1,200 pounds can be used to advantage. All depends upon the condition of the soil and its previous treatment, especially with regard to the manure and fertilizers used upon it during the preceding two or three years.

Commercial fertilizers as a rule should be applied either a few days before planting or at the time the crops are planted. The usual practice is to plow the land and give it its first harrowing, then spread the fertilizer from a pail or with a fertilizer distributor, harrowing the soil two or three times to get it in proper condition and at the same time mixing the fertilizer with it. For crops like potatoes and sweetpotatoes it is customary to scatter the fertilizer in the rows, taking care to mix it thoroughly with the soil before the seed is dropped, or, in the case of sweetpotatoes, before the ridges are thrown up.

The roots of most garden crops spread to considerable distances. The application of fertilizer to the entire area, therefore, will provide a uniform source of food for the plants to feed on. Care must be taken not to place fertilizer too near seedlings or young plants, as burning of the roots is likely to occur. Like caution must be exercised in using nitrate of soda or sulphate of ammonia as a side dressing for growing crops. On a half-acre garden 75 to 100 pounds of any of these concentrated sources of nitrogen is sufficient for one application, and where only a part of the garden is treated the quantity should be regulated accordingly. The fertilizer should be sown alongside the rows and cultivated into the topsoil.

### LIME

Lime improves the texture of certain heavy soils, but its excessive use may prove injurious to most garden crops. As a general rule, asparagus, celery, beets, spinach, and sometimes carrots are benefited by the moderate use of lime, especially on soils that are naturally deficient in lime. Most of the garden vegetables do best on soils that are slightly acid, and all vegetables are injured by the application of lime in excess of their requirement. For this reason lime should be applied only where it is definitely shown by actual test to be necessary, and in no case should it be applied in large quantities. As a matter of fact most garden soils in a state of high fertility do not require the addition of lime. With good drainage, plenty of manure in the soil, and the moderate use of commercial fertilizers, the growth requirements of nearly all vegetables may be fully met.

Where lime is applied, it should be spread after plowing and be well mixed with the topsoil by harrowing. It should not be applied at the same time as, or mixed with, commercial fertilizers or manure, as the chemical changes that take place result in the loss of nitrogen and thus destroy the effectiveness of the fertilizers. As a rule, lime

---

[2] There are 43,560 square feet in an acre, or an area each of the four sides of which measures approximately 208½ feet. A piece of land 208 feet in length and 105 feet in width will contain practically one-half acre. A piece of land 220 feet in length and 100 feet in width will also contain practically one-half acre.

should not be applied in the fall, as it leaches from the soil during the winter. Any of the various forms of lime, such as hydrated lime and air-slaked lime, may be used. In some cases the unburned but finely ground limerock is used, but its action is slower than that of the burned lime. Finely ground oyster shells and marl are frequently used as substitutes for lime. Owing to its influence on the development of potato scab, lime should not be used on land that is being planted to potatoes.

### SOIL PREPARATION

The time and method of preparing the garden for planting depend on the type of soil and location. Heavy clay soils in the northern sections are frequently benefited by fall plowing and exposure to freezing and thawing during the winter. Gardens in the dry-land areas should be plowed and leveled in the fall, so that the soil will absorb and retain all moisture that falls during the winter. The sandy soils of the South as a rule should not be plowed until near the time of planting. Wherever there is a heavy growth of crabgrass or a green cover crop the land should be plowed well in advance of planting and the soil disked several times to aid in the decay and incorporation of this material. Soils on which gardens are ordinarily planted should not be plowed or worked while wet. Sandy soils generally bear plowing a trifle sooner than heavy clay soils. The usual test is to squeeze together a handful of soil. If it adheres in a ball and does not readily crumble when slight pressure is exerted by the thumb and finger, it is too wet for plowing or working.

Fall-plowed land may be prepared as a rule by disking and harrowing. Spring-plowed land should be harrowed immediately after plowing, and if the soil is inclined to be lumpy a plank drag or a roller should be used for pulverizing it. Seeds grow more readily on a fine well-prepared soil than on a coarse or lumpy one, and thorough preparation greatly reduces the work of planting and caring for the crops. Spading is sometimes advisable in preparing small areas, such as beds for extra early crops of lettuce, onions, beets, and carrots, but the main portion of the garden should be plowed and harrowed. As a rule the tools ordinarily used on the farm will be suitable for preparing the garden for planting. In laying out the garden provision should be made for a gate or opening through which to haul manure or to bring in teams or a tractor as well as the tools for preparing and cultivating the garden.

### PLAN AND ARRANGEMENT

It would be difficult to give a plan or specific arrangement for a garden that would suit all demands. Such a plan must be devised by each individual grower. Suggestive arrangements, however, are here presented, with the idea that they can readily be changed to suit local conditions.

The first consideration in planning the arrangement of a garden is the kind of cultivation that is to be employed. When the work is to be done mainly by means of horse tools the site and the arrangement should be such as to give the longest possible rows, and straight lines should be followed. (Fig. 1.) The garden should be free from

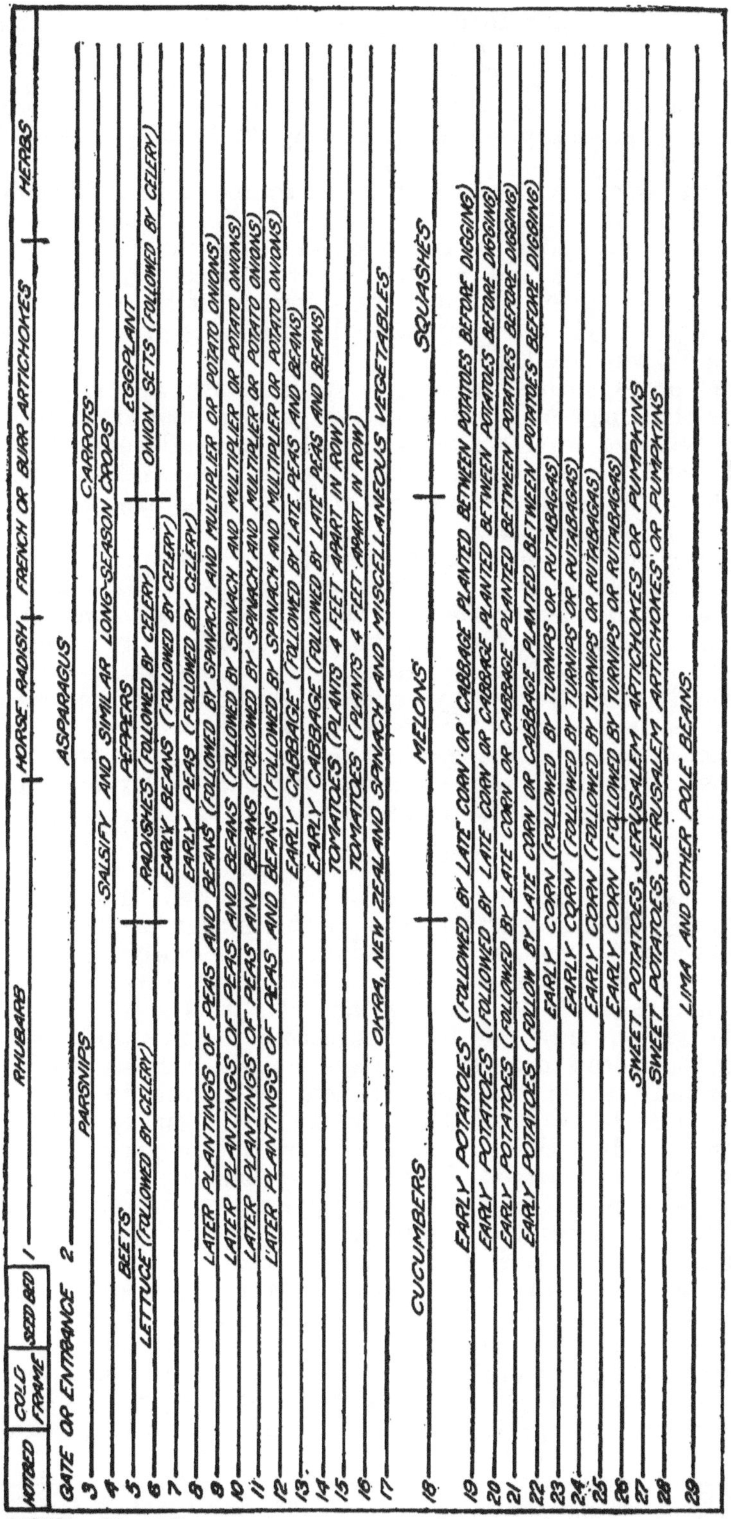
HOTBED
COLD FRAME
SEED BED
1 RHUBARB
HORSE RADISH
FRENCH OR BURR ARTICHOKES
HERBS
GATE OR ENTRANCE 2
ASPARAGUS
3 PARSNIPS
CARROTS
4 SALSIFY AND SIMILAR LONG-SEASON CROPS
5 BEETS
PEPPERS
EGGPLANT
6 LETTUCE (FOLLOWED BY CELERY)
RADISHES (FOLLOWED BY CELERY)
ONION SETS (FOLLOWED BY CELERY)
7 EARLY BEANS (FOLLOWED BY CELERY)
8 EARLY PEAS (FOLLOWED BY CELERY)
9 LATER PLANTINGS OF PEAS AND BEANS (FOLLOWED BY SPINACH AND MULTIPLIER OR POTATO ONIONS)
10 LATER PLANTINGS OF PEAS AND BEANS (FOLLOWED BY SPINACH AND MULTIPLIER OR POTATO ONIONS)
11 LATER PLANTINGS OF PEAS AND BEANS (FOLLOWED BY SPINACH AND MULTIPLIER OR POTATO ONIONS)
12 LATER PLANTINGS OF PEAS AND BEANS (FOLLOWED BY SPINACH AND MULTIPLIER OR POTATO ONIONS)
13 EARLY CABBAGE (FOLLOWED BY LATE PEAS AND BEANS)
14 EARLY CABBAGE (FOLLOWED BY LATE PEAS AND BEANS)
15 TOMATOES (PLANTS 4 FEET APART IN ROW)
16 TOMATOES (PLANTS 4 FEET APART IN ROW)
17 OKRA, NEW ZEALAND SPINACH AND MISCELLANEOUS VEGETABLES
18 CUCUMBERS
MELONS
SQUASHES
19 EARLY POTATOES (FOLLOWED BY LATE CORN OR CABBAGE PLANTED BETWEEN POTATOES BEFORE DIGGING)
20 EARLY POTATOES (FOLLOWED BY LATE CORN OR CABBAGE PLANTED BETWEEN POTATOES BEFORE DIGGING)
21 EARLY POTATOES (FOLLOWED BY LATE CORN OR CABBAGE PLANTED BETWEEN POTATOES BEFORE DIGGING)
22 EARLY POTATOES (FOLLOW BY LATE CORN OR CABBAGE PLANTED BETWEEN POTATOES BEFORE DIGGING)
23 EARLY CORN (FOLLOWED BY TURNIPS OR RUTABAGAS)
24 EARLY CORN (FOLLOWED BY TURNIPS OR RUTABAGAS)
25 EARLY CORN (FOLLOWED BY TURNIPS OR RUTABAGAS)
26 EARLY CORN (FOLLOWED BY TURNIPS OR RUTABAGAS)
27 SWEET POTATOES, JERUSALEM ARTICHOKES OR PUMPKINS
28 SWEET POTATOES, JERUSALEM ARTICHOKES OR PUMPKINS
29 LIMA AND OTHER POLE BEANS.

**FIGURE 1.**—Plan of a half-acre garden. Length, 220 feet; width, 100 feet. A half-acre garden will produce all the vegetables the average family can use throughout the growing season and a surplus for canning, storing, and drying

64902°—31——2

paths across the rows, and turning spaces should be provided at the ends. For hand cultivation the arrangement can be quite different, as the garden may be laid off in sections, with transverse walks, and the rows for most crops may be much closer. Horse cultivation is recommended whenever possible, as it very materially lessens the labor and cost of caring for the crops.

Where there is any great variation in the composition of the soil in different parts of the garden it will be advisable to take this into consideration when arranging for the location of the various crops. If a part of the land is low and moist, such crops as celery, onions, and late cucumbers should be placed there. If part of the soil is high, warm, and dry, there is the proper location for early crops and those that need quick, warm soil.

Permanent crops, such as asparagus and rhubarb, also any of the small fruits that may be planted in the garden, should be located where they will not interfere with the plowing and cultivation of the annual crops. If a hotbed, a coldframe, or a special seed bed is provided, it should be either in one corner of the garden or located outside of the garden entirely.

Tall-growing crops should be so located that they will not shade or interfere with the growth of the smaller crops. There seems to be little choice as to whether the rows run east and west or north and south, but they should conform to the general shape of the garden with convenience of cultivation in mind. In general, the smaller crops, especially those worked by hand, should be located nearest the house, with the larger crops like potatoes, sweet corn, and the vine crops in that portion of the garden most distant from the house. However, the general location of crops will depend largely on the character of the soil and convenience in cultivating.

### SEED SUPPLY

Seeds for the farm garden should be ordered well in advance of planting time. Make a plan (fig. 1) of the garden, indicating the space each crop is to have, and order the seeds accordingly, allowing for replanting in case of a poor stand due to adverse weather conditions or other causes.[3] In making the plan it is a good idea to measure the garden carefully to be sure that the required space is available for each crop included. It pays to use garden seeds of high quality, especially those bred and selected for disease resistance.

Seeds saved at home from the previous year's garden should be carefully inspected so that in case they are not in good condition fresh ones may be ordered. In estimating the supply, allowance should always be made for two or more plantings of certain vegetables and for the tastes and requirements of the different members of the family. After careful checking to see that the order has been completely filled, the seeds should be stored in a dry place at a temperature 10 to 15 degrees below that of the average living room until planting time. A tin box or a large tin can makes a suitable container for storing vegetable seeds, especially as it gives protection from mice. Seeds of many of the garden vegetables will keep from four to six years if properly stored, while others lose their vitality quickly.

---

[3] The approximate quantities of seed that should be provided for planting a garden to supply vegetables for a family of five or six persons are given in the table on page 22.

THE FARM GARDEN 9

#### STARTING EARLY PLANTS

Under southern conditions practically all vegetable plants may be started in specially prepared beds in the open with little or no covering. In the middle section and throughout the North and West, if an early garden is desired, it is essential that certain crops such as tomatoes, peppers, eggplant, cabbage, and cauliflower, and occasionally lettuce, onions, beets, cucumbers, squashes, and melons, be started indoors or in coldframes.

#### THE SEED BOX IN THE HOUSE

The simplest method of growing early plants is to provide a flat tray or box, such as is shown in Figure 2, which may be fitted into a south window of any room that is kept reasonably warm. Fill this

FIGURE 2.—Window box for starting early plants in the house

box with sifted soil, and in it sow the seeds of tomato, eggplant, peppers, and cabbage. When the plants are 10 to 20 days old, they can be transplanted to other boxes filled with reasonably rich sifted soil from the compost pile. Plants grown in this manner in the house, however, are inclined to be spindling, and better results may be obtained where a hotbed or a coldframe is employed.

#### HOTBEDS AND COLDFRAMES

In the South the hotbed will not be necessary as a rule, but a coldframe or sash-covered pit on the south side of a building will be found satisfactory for starting the early plants. In colder sections some form of heat is essential, and a manure-heated hotbed is usually the best type to provide. In the North the hotbed should be started in February or early in March, in order that the plants may be well grown in time to plant in the open ground.

The hotbed should always face the south and should be located on the south side of a building, a tight board fence, or a protecting wall, preferably near the house, where it can be given proper attention. A hotbed consists of a pit about 18 inches deep filled with fermenting horse-stable manure to furnish the heat. Material that is about half manure and half straw bedding is desirable. Place the manure in a low, flat pile, and turn it over once or twice as it begins to heat, in order to have it uniform; then place it in the hotbed pit in thin layers, shaking the manure out loosely as it is spread. Each successive layer, as it is put in, should be well trampled, and, if dry, a small quantity of water added so that the manure will pack solidly in the pit.

After the manure has been properly leveled and trampled in the bed, the frame to support the sash is placed in position. Generally the frame is made to carry four or five standard hotbed sash, or where only a small bed is required, one to three sash. The front or south side of the frame should be 8 to 12 inches lower than the back, in order to get the greatest benefit from the sunlight and so that water will drain from the glass. From 3 to 5 inches of good screened garden loam or specially prepared soil from the compost heap is then spread evenly over the manure in the frame, the sash are put on, and the bed is allowed to heat. At first the temperature of the bed will run somewhat high, but no seeds should be planted until the soil temperature falls below 80° F., which in most cases will be in about three or four days. It is not safe to judge the temperature by feeling the soil with the hand. A thermometer, its bulb buried in the soil, is the best means of telling when the bed falls to the proper temperature.

Standard hotbed sash in common use are 3 by 6 feet, containing three to five rows of glass. The sash may be purchased unpainted and unglazed or fully painted and filled with glass as desired. They should have at least two coats of paint consisting of white lead and linseed oil. In glazing the sash the glass should be bedded in putty, the panes overlapping about one-fourth inch and fastened securely in place with zinc glazing nails made for the purpose. No putty should be placed on the surface of the glass, the glass being simply bedded in putty and all surplus putty trimmed off.

In the colder parts of the country, board shutters, straw, or burlap mats, in addition to the sash, will be required as a covering during cold nights. It is also desirable to have a supply of straw or loose manure on hand to throw over the bed in extremely cold weather.

On bright days, when the hotbed heats very quickly from the sunshine on the glass, the sash should be raised slightly on the side opposite from the wind. In ventilating, care should be taken to protect the plants from a direct draft of cold air. Toward evening the sash should be closed, in order that the bed may become sufficiently warm before nightfall. Hotbeds should be watered on bright days, preferably in the morning. If it is necessary to water late in the day, the sash should be left open for a short time until the plants dry off. Plants grown in hotbeds are frequently lost by a disease known as damping off, which can be largely prevented by careful watering and proper ventilation.

Coldframes are constructed like hotbeds, except that no manure or other heating material is used. (Fig. 3.) They are covered with ordinary hotbed sash, but cotton cloth may be substituted for the sash. In the South coldframes are used for growing early plants; in the North they are used for hardening off plants that have been started in hotbeds or in the house. The same general rules for the care of a hotbed apply to a coldframe, but the latter is usually

FIGURE 3.—A sash-covered frame (coldframe) for starting early plants

ventilated more freely. Toward the close of the plant-growing period the sash or cloth covering of the frame may be left off entirely,

FIGURE 4.—Methods of starting early plants for the garden indoors by the use of (A) quart berry boxes and (B) paper bands

to adapt the plants to outdoor conditions, but the covering should be kept near by in case of a sudden drop in temperature.

### SPECIAL METHODS FOR STARTING EARLY PLANTS

Early plants for the garden may be started indoors in quart berry boxes (fig. 4, A), paper drinking cups, paper bands (fig. 4, B), or in regular clay flowerpots. The containers are filled with sifted soil and placed in the hotbed, or if in the house they are placed in a shallow box. A small amount of seed is sown in each container, and after the plants are well under way they are transferred to the garden, the container usually being removed from about the roots of the plants when set in the planting hole. In the case of clay flowerpots the ball of earth containing the roots is simply jarred loose and removed from the pot. Soft paper bands or peat pots need not be removed, the roots of the plants being simply allowed to grow through the container and into the soil about them.

Market gardeners generally spot the plants in the hotbed or coldframe 4 or 5 inches apart in each direction. In moving them to the garden a knife is run to a depth of 4 or 5 inches in each direction between the plants, cutting the soil in blocks as shown in Figure 5. Each block, with the plant in its center, is removed direct to the garden. Plants moved in this manner should be watered when set, unless the soil is very moist.

FIGURE 5.—Tomato plant for the early garden, grown in hotbed or coldframe by the blocking method

### SOUTHERN-GROWN PLANTS

Southern vegetable plants grown in the open and shipped to all parts of the country are now to a considerable degree taking the place of the plants formerly grown locally in hotbeds, coldframes, and special seed beds. These plants are grown very cheaply and withstand transplanting remarkably well. They may not in all cases be as good as home-grown plants, but they save the trouble of starting plants in the house or in a hotbed, and when planted they usually grow very rapidly. The disadvantages of using these plants are the occasional delay in obtaining them and the possibility of transmitting certain diseases, such as the wilt disease of the tomato, black rot of cabbage, and diseases caused by nematodes, which are common on various crops in the South. Southern-grown plants are now offered for sale by most of the northern seedsmen and often by local hardware and supply houses.

### TRANSPLANTING

Plants started in the house or in hotbeds should be transplanted to give them more room about the time the first true leaves are formed. The small plants may be transplanted to flat boxes or to the coldframe to stand 2 to 5 inches apart each way. Where clay flowerpots or any of the containers mentioned are used, and a single plant is set in each container, excellent early plants may be grown, with the advantage that the roots will not be disturbed when they are set in the garden. Toward the end of the protected period the plants should be exposed more and more to outdoor conditions. Such plants usually withstand transfer to the garden with little check and few losses. Plants while undergoing the hardening process should be watered sparingly, but just before they are moved to the garden they should be given a thorough watering.

When the time comes to set the plants in the open ground, everything should be in readiness, the soil in good condition, and water available for watering the plants in case there is not enough moisture in the soil. Plants grown in the coldframe or in specially prepared seed beds should be lifted carefully with a trowel or a spade, as much soil being kept on their roots as possible. Plants do best if moved on a cloudy day or just before a rain, or late in the evening. In using water when setting out plants, first set the plant in the hole and partly fill the hole with soil; next apply the water, allowing it

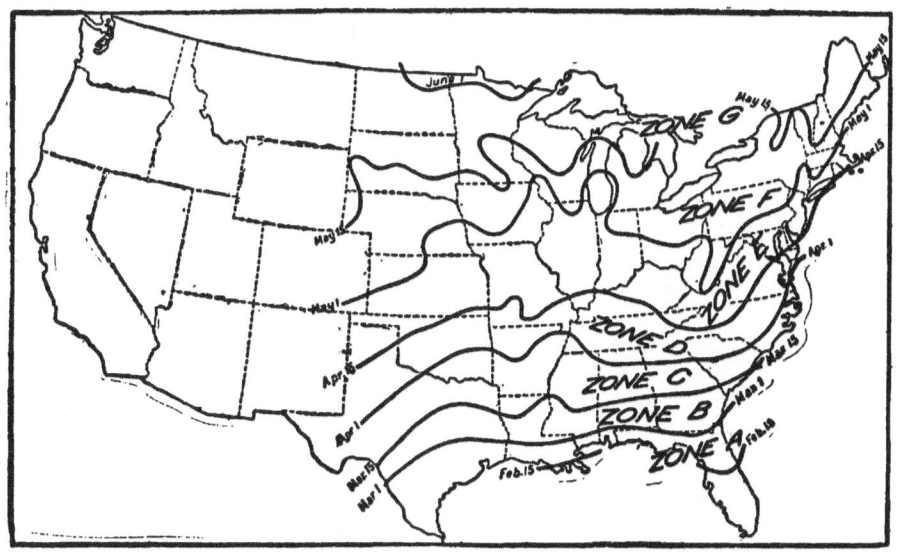

FIGURE 6.—A zone map of the United States, based on the average dates of the latest killing frost in spring east of the Rocky Mountains

to soak well into the soil. Then fill around the plant with the drier soil, and firm it about the plants. Plants set in this manner seldom wilt. When setting a small number of plants in the garden during a dry period it is often possible to protect them from the midday sun by setting a shingle or a small piece of board at a slant on the south side of each plant. If the plants are protected thus for two or three days after setting, few of them will be lost.

Cabbage and other vegetable plants that are moved direct from the seed bed should be carefully lifted by running a trowel or a spade beneath them, as much soil as possible being left on their roots. Plants handled in this manner should be set either when there is an abundance of moisture in the soil or just before a rain, with the soil firmly packed about their roots. If the soil is dry, a pint or more of water should be poured about the roots of each plant.

### TIME OF PLANTING

The earliest dates for planting the various vegetables depend upon the locality, beginning during December or January in the extreme South and following the advance of the season northward until approximately June 10 in the extreme North. Garden crops may be divided into four groups: Crops that can be planted before the time of the last killing frost in the spring, those that can be planted about the time the last killing frost is expected, those that can not be planted until danger of frost is past, and those that can not be planted until the ground and the weather are warm. The zone map shown in Figure 6 is applicable to that portion of the United States east of the Rocky Mountains and is based on the dates of the last killing frost in the spring. This map and Table 1 furnish a reasonably safe guide, although conditions may vary from year to year. There is also a difference of several days within the zones themselves, owing to elevation and proximity to bodies of water.

TABLE 1.—*Earliest safe dates for planting vegetable seeds in the open in the zones of the United States illustrated in Figure 6*

| Crop | Zone A | Zone B | Zone C | Zone D | Zone E | Zone F | Zone G |
|---|---|---|---|---|---|---|---|
| Asparagus | | Feb. 1 to Mar. 1 | Mar. 1 to 15 | Mar. 15 to Apr. 15 | Apr. 15 to May 1 | May 1 to 15 | May 15 to June 1. |
| Beans: | | | | | | | |
| Lima | Mar. 1 to 15 | Mar. 15 to Apr. 1 | Apr. 1 to 15 | May 1 to 15 | May 15 to June 1 | May 15 to June 15 | May 15 to June 15. |
| Snap | Feb. 15 to Mar. 1 | Mar. 1 to 15 | Mar. 15 to 30 | Apr. 1 to May 1 | May 1 to 15 | May 1 to June 1 | May 15 to June 1. |
| Beet | Feb. 1 to 15 | Feb. 15 to Mar. 1 | Mar. 1 to 15 | Mar. 15 to Apr. 15 | Apr. 15 to May 1 | May 1 to 15 | May 15 to June 1. |
| Broccoli: | | | | | | | |
| Heading [1] | Jan. 1 to Feb. 1 | Jan. 15 to Feb. 15 | Feb. 15 to Mar. 1 | Mar. 1 to 15 | Mar. 15 to Apr. 15 | Apr. 15 to May 1 | May 1 to 15. |
| Sprouting [1] | do | do | do | do | do | do | Do. |
| Brussels sprouts | do | do | do | do | do | do | Do. |
| Cabbage | do | do | do | do | do | do | Do. |
| Cabbage, Chinese | do | do | do | do | do | do | Do. |
| Cardoon | do | do | do | do | do | do | Do. |
| Carrot | Feb. 1 to 15 | Feb. 15 to Mar. 1 | Mar. 1 to 15 | Mar. 15 to Apr. 1 | Apr. 15 to May 1 | May 1 to 15 | May 1 to June 1. |
| Cauliflower [1] | Jan. 1 to Feb. 1 | Jan. 15 to Feb. 15 | Feb. 15 to Mar. 1 | Mar. 1 to 15 | Mar. 15 to Apr. 15 | Apr. 15 to May 1 | May 1 to 15. |
| Celeriac | do | do | do | do | do | do | Do. |
| Celery [1] | do | do | do | do | do | do | Do. |
| Chard | do | do | do | do | do | do | Do. |
| Chervil | do | do | do | do | do | do | Do. |
| Chicory, witloof | Jan. 1 to Feb. 1 | Feb. 1 to 15 | Feb. 15 to Mar. 1 | Mar. 1 to 15 | June 1 to 15 | June 15 to July 1 | June 15 to July 1. |
| Chives | do | do | do | do | Mar. 15 to May 1 | Apr. 1 to May 1 | May 1 to 15. |
| Collards [1] | Feb. 1 to 15 | Feb. 15 to Mar. 1 | Mar. 1 to 15 | Mar. 15 to Apr. 15 | Apr. 1 to May 1 | May 1 to June 1 | May 15 to June 1. |
| Corn salad | Feb. 15 to Mar. 1 | Mar. 1 to 15 | Mar. 15 to Apr. 1 | Apr. 1 to May 1 | Apr. 15 to May 15 | May 1 to June 1 | May 15 to June 15. |
| Corn, sweet | | | | | | | |
| Cress: | | | | | | | |
| Upland | Feb. 1 to 15 | Feb. 15 to Mar. 1 | Mar. 1 to 15 | Mar. 15 to Apr. 1 | Apr. 1 to May 1 | May 1 to 15 | May 15 to June 1. |
| Water | Mar. 1 to 15 | Mar. 15 to Apr. 1 | Apr. 1 to 15 | do | do | do | Do. |
| Cucumber | Jan. 1 to Feb. 1 | Jan. 15 to Feb. 15 | Feb. 1 to Mar. 15 | Apr. 15 to May 1 | May 1 to June 1 | May 15 to June 15 | June 1 to 15. |
| Dandelion | Mar. 1 to Apr. 1 | Mar. 15 to Apr. 15 | Apr. 15 to May 15 | Mar. 15 to Apr. 15 | May 1 to June 1 | May 1 to 15 | Do. |
| Dasheen | Feb. 1 to 15 | Feb. 15 to Mar. 1 | Mar. 1 to 15 | Mar. 15 to Apr. 1 | Apr. 15 to May 1 | May 1 to 15 | June 1 to 15. |
| Eggplant [1] | Jan. 1 to Feb. 1 | Feb. 1 to 15 | Feb. 15 to Apr. 1 | Apr. 1 to 15 | Apr. 15 to May 1 | Apr. 1 to May 1 | Do. |
| Endive | | | | | | | |
| Florence fennel | Feb. 1 to 15 | Feb. 15 to Mar. 1 | Mar. 1 to 15 | Mar. 15 to Apr. 1 | Mar. 15 to Apr. 15 | May 1 to 15 | May 15 to June 1. |
| Garlic | Jan. 1 to Feb. 1 | Feb. 1 to 15 | Feb. 15 to Apr. 1 | Mar. 1 to 15 | Mar. 15 to Apr. 15 | Apr. 1 to May 1 | May 15 to June 1. |
| Horseradish [1] | Jan. 1 to Feb. 1 | Feb. 1 to 15 | Feb. 15 to Mar. 1 | Mar. 1 to 15 | Mar. 15 to Apr. 15 | Apr. 15 to May 1 | May 1 to June 1. |
| Jerusalem artichoke | do | do | do | do | do | do | Do. |
| Kale | Feb. 1 to 15 | Feb. 15 to Mar. 1 | Feb. 15 to Mar. 1 | Mar. 15 to Apr. 1 | Mar. 15 to Apr. 15 | May 1 to 15 | May 15 to June 1. |
| Kohlrabi | Jan. 1 to Feb. 1 | Feb. 1 to 15 | Feb. 15 to Mar. 1 | Mar. 1 to 15 | Mar. 15 to Apr. 15 | Apr. 1 to May 1 | May 1 to 15. |
| Leek | Feb. 1 to 15 | Feb. 15 to Mar. 1 | Mar. 1 to 15 | Mar. 15 to Apr. 15 | Mar. 15 to Apr. 15 | Apr. 15 to May 15 | May 15 to June 1. |
| Lettuce | Mar. 1 to 16 | Mar. 15 to Apr. 1 | Apr. 1 to 15 | Mar. 15 to Apr. 15 | May 1 to June 1 | June 1 to 15 | May 15 to June 1. |
| Martynia | | | | | | | |
| Muskmelon | Feb. 1 to 16 | Feb. 15 to Mar. 1 | Mar. 1 to 15 | Mar. 15 to Apr. 15 | Apr. 1 to May 1 | May 1 to 15 | May 15 to June 1. |
| Mustard | | | | | | | |
| Okra | Feb. 15 to Mar. 1 | Mar. 1 to 15 | Mar. 15 to 30 | Apr. 15 to May 1 | May 1 to 15 | May 15 to June 1 | May 15 to June 1. |

[1] Plants.

TABLE 1.—*Earliest safe dates for planting vegetable seeds in the open in the zones of the United States illustrated in Figure 6*—Continued.

| Crop | Zone A | Zone B | Zone C | Zone D | Zone E | Zone F | Zone G |
|---|---|---|---|---|---|---|---|
| Onion: | | | | | | | |
|   Plants | Jan. 1 to Feb. 1 | Feb. 1 to 15 | Feb. 15 to Mar. 1 | Mar. 1 to 15 | Mar. 15 to Apr. 15 | Apr. 1 to May 1 | May 1 to 15. |
|   Seed | Feb. 1 to 15 | Feb. 15 to Mar. 1 | Mar. 1 to 15 | Mar. 15 to Apr. 1 | Apr. 1 to May 1 | May 1 to 15 | May 15 to June 1. |
|   Sets | Jan. 1 to Feb. 1 | Feb. 1 to 15 | Feb. 15 to Mar. 1 | Mar. 1 to 15 | Mar. 15 to Apr. 15 | Apr. 1 to May 1 | May 1 to 15. |
| Parsley | Feb. 1 to 15 | Feb. 15 to Mar. 1 | Mar. 1 to 15 | Mar. 15 to Apr. 1 | Apr. 1 to May 1 | May 1 to 15 | May 15 to June 1. |
| Parsley, turnip-rooted | do | do | do | do | do | do | Do. |
| Parsnip | | | | | | | Do. |
| Peas | Jan. 1 to Feb. 1 | Feb. 1 to 15 | Feb. 15 to Mar. 1 | Mar. 1 to 15 | Mar. 15 to Apr. 15 | Apr. 15 to May 1 | May 1 to June 1. |
| Peppers [1] | Mar. 1 to 15 | Mar. 15 to Apr. 1 | Apr. 1 to 15 | Apr. 15 to May 1 | May 1 to June 1 | June 1 to 15 | June 1 to 15. |
| Physalis | do | do | do | do | do | do | May 1 to 15. |
| Poke | | | | Mar. 1 to 15 | Mar. 15 to Apr. 15 | Apr. 15 to May 1 | May 1 to June 1. |
| Potato | Jan. 1 to Feb. 1 | Feb. 1 to 15 | Feb. 15 to Mar. 1 | Apr. 15 to May 1 | May 1 to June 1 | June 1 to 15 | |
| Pumpkin | Mar. 1 to 15 | Mar. 15 to Apr. 1 | Apr. 1 to 15 | Mar. 1 to 15 | Mar. 15 to Apr. 15 | Apr. 15 to May 1 | May 1 to 15. |
| Radish | Jan. 1 to Feb. 1 | Feb. 1 to 15 | Feb. 15 to Mar. 1 | Mar. 15 to Apr. 15 | Apr. 1 to May 1 | May 1 to 15 | May 15 to June 1. |
| Rhubarb [1] | | | | | Apr. 15 to May 1 | Apr. 15 to May 15 | May 1 to 15. |
| Salsify | Feb. 1 to 15 | Feb. 15 to Mar. 1 | Mar. 1 to 15 | Mar. 1 to 15 | Mar. 15 to Apr. 15 | Apr. 1 to May 1 | May 1 to 15. |
| Shallots | Jan. 1 to Feb. 1 | Feb. 1 to 15 | Feb. 15 to Mar. 1 | Mar. 1 to Apr. 1 | Apr. 1 to 15 | Apr. 15 to May 1 | Do. |
| Sorrel | Feb. 1 to Mar. 1 | Feb. 15 to Mar. 15 | Mar. 1 to Apr. 1 | May 1 to 15 | May 15 to June 1 | May 15 to June 15 | May 1 to 15. |
| Spinach | Feb. 1 to 15 | Feb. 15 to Apr. 1 | Mar. 1 to 15 | do | May 15 to June 1 | June 1 to 15 | June 1 to 15. |
| Spinach, New Zealand | Mar. 1 to 15 | Mar. 15 to Apr. 1 | Apr. 1 to 15 | do | May 1 to June 1 | May 15 to June 15 | |
| Squash | do | do | do | May 1 to 15 | May 1 to June 1 | June 1 to 15 | |
| Sweetpotato [1] | do | do | do | Apr. 15 to May 1 | do | do | |
| Tomato [1] | Jan. 1 to Feb. 1 | Feb. 1 to 15 | Feb. 15 to Mar. 1 | Mar. 1 to 15 | Mar. 15 to Apr. 15 | Apr. 15 to May 1 | June 15 to 30. |
| Turnip greens | do | do | do | do | do | do | May 1 to 15. |
| Turnips and rutabagas | Mar. 1 to 15 | Mar. 15 to Apr. 1 | Apr. 1 to 15 | Apr. 15 to May 1 | May 1 to June 1 | June 1 to 15 | Do. |
| Watermelon | | | | | | | |

[1] Plants.

By referring to Figure 7 it will be noted that the dates when the last killing frost may be expected in the western part of the country are extremely variable. For example, at certain points in Colorado this date is as late as June 12 or 16; at points in Wyoming to the northward it is as early as May 4; in California there is a variation from January 25 to June 22; and in Arizona, from February 15 to

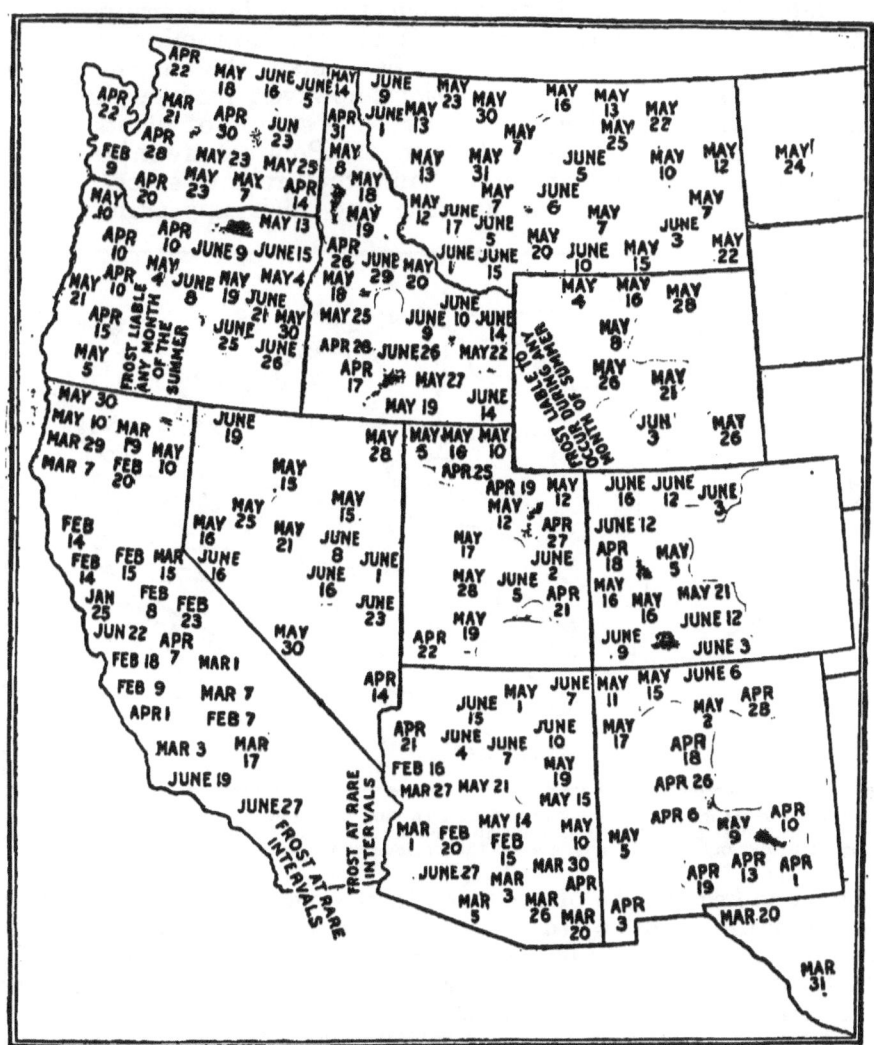

FIGURE 7.—Outline map showing the average date of the last killing frost in spring in the western portion of the United States

June 27. Primarily these variations are owing to differences in the elevations of the stations where the observations were made rather than to the location of the stations in different zones.

Of equal importance are the latest dates on which various crops may be planted and yet mature before the earliest killing frost in the autumn. The zone map shown in Figure 8 gives the approximate dates of the earliest autumn frosts in the central and eastern part of the United States, while the outline map shown in Figure 9 gives this information for the Rocky Mountain and Pacific coast regions. It will be noted that in the latter area there is one section where frost rarely ever occurs and two sections where frost is liable to occur during any month of the year. By referring to Table 2 the approximate latest date for planting any given crop may be determined.

Most farmers know by experience and by the blossoming of certain native trees when it is reasonably safe to plant the various garden crops. Exceptional seasonal variations, however, are likely to occur, and it is always desirable to have a reserve supply of plants for replanting in case the first are lost by frost. Potatoes are injured even by moderate frost. On the other hand, they require a considerable period between the time of planting and their appearance above

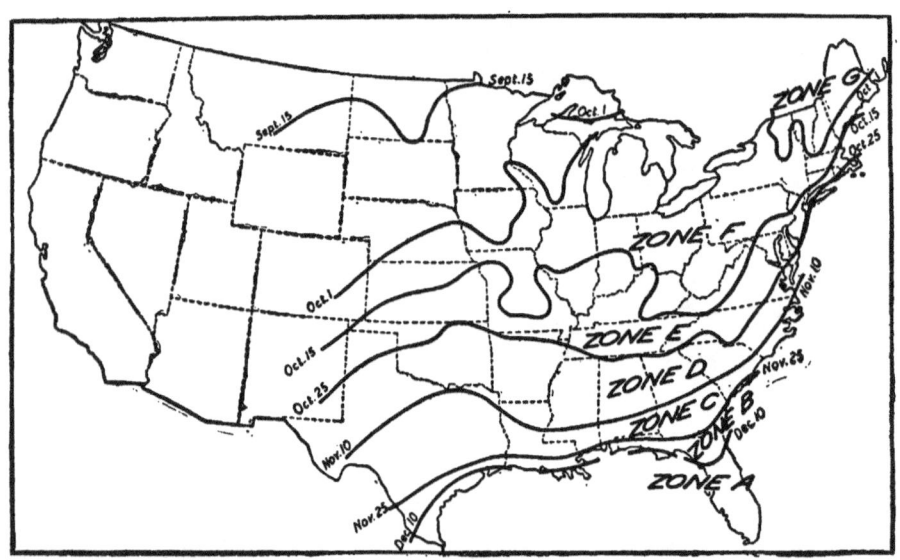

FIGURE 8.—Zone map of the central and eastern part of the United States based on average date of first killing frost in autumn. By referring to Table 2 the latest safe date for planting any crop in any one of the various zones may be determined

ground, and so may be planted well in advance of the date on which the last killing frost of the season may be expected. Potatoes that are just above ground can often be saved from frost by covering the plants with soil. Peas, onions, cabbage, kale, spinach, turnips, and beets will stand considerable frost. It frequently pays to take a reasonable chance of putting them in fairly early. If they are not killed, it means early vegetables; if they are, nothing is lost but the seed and the labor of replanting. Summer squashes, cucumbers, and melons frequently may be planted in advance of their normal season, the hills being protected from wind and frost by paper or glass covers. In addition these covers protect the plants from insects.

### PLANTING THE GARDEN

Methods of planting garden crops vary with the locality and the type of soil. In some sections of the South, especially along the

South Atlantic coast and in the Gulf States, it may be necessary to plant on beds or ridges in order to obtain good drainage. Level planting is recommended on the lighter sandy soils and on the majority of the sandy loam and clay loam soils of the North and North-

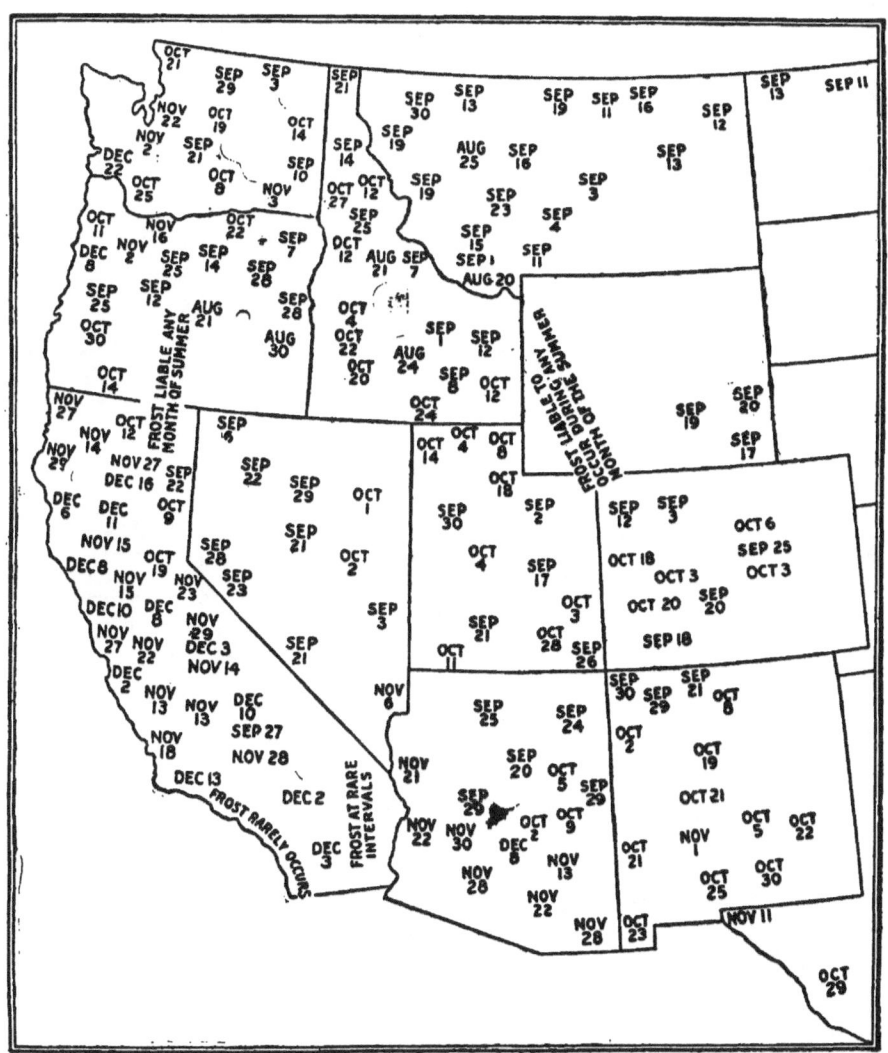

FIGURE 9.—Outline map showing average date of first killing frost in the autumn in the western portion of the United States

east. In the irrigated sections of the West the seeds are usually planted on the side of the furrows a little above the irrigation water level. In all cases the method of planting should conform to the approved customs of the region and the type of soil upon which the garden is located.

TABLE 2.—*Latest safe dates for planting vegetable seeds and plants in the open in the zones of the United States illustrated in Figure 8*

| Crop | Zone A | Zone B | Zone C | Zone D | Zone E | Zone F | Zone G |
|---|---|---|---|---|---|---|---|
| Asparagus | | Nov. 1 to Dec. 1 | Nov. 1 to Dec. 1 | Nov. 1 to Dec. 1 | Nov. 1 to Dec. 1 | Oct. 15 to Nov. 15 | Oct. 1 to Nov. 1 |
| Beans: | | | | | | | |
| Lima | Oct. 1 | Oct. 15 | Sept. 1 | Aug. 15 | Aug. 1 | Aug. 15 | Aug. 15 |
| Snap | do | do | do | do | do | July 15 | July 1 |
| Beet | Nov. 1 | Oct. 1 | do | do | do | do | Do. |
| Broccoli: | | | | | | | |
| Heading [1] | do | do | do | do | Aug. 1 | July 15 | Do. |
| Sprouting [1] | do | do | do | do | do | do | Do. |
| Brussels sprouts | do | do | do | do | do | Aug. 1 | Do. |
| Cabbage [1] | do | do | do | Sept. 1 | July 15 | July 15 | Do. |
| Cabbage, Chinese | do | do | Oct. 1 | Aug. 15 | Aug. 1 | July 15 | Do. |
| Cardoon | do | do | Sept. 1 | do | do | Aug. 1 | Do. |
| Carrot | do | do | do | do | do | do | Do. |
| Cauliflower [1] | do | do | Oct. 1 | Sept. 1 | Aug. 1 | July 1 | June 15 |
| Celeriac | Nov. 1 | Oct. 1 | do | do | July 15 | do | Do. |
| Celery [1] | do | do | do | do | do | do | Do. |
| Chard | do | do | do | do | do | do | Do. |
| Chervil | Dec. 1 | Nov. 1 | do | Aug. 15 | June 15 | June 1 | May 15 |
| Chicory, witloof | | | | July 1 | July 15 | July 1 | June 1 |
| Chives | Nov. 1 | Oct. 15 | Sept. 1 | Aug. 15 | Sept. 15 | Aug. 15 | July 15 |
| Collards [1] | Dec. 1 | Nov. 15 | Nov. 1 | Oct. 1 | | July 1 | June 15 |
| Corn salad | Oct. 1 | Sept. 1 | Aug. 15 | Aug. 1 | Sept. 15 | | |
| Corn, sweet | | | | | | Sept. 1 | |
| Cress: | | | | | | do | |
| Upland | Dec. 1 | Nov. 15 | Nov. 1 | Oct. 15 | Oct. 1 | July 15 | June 1 |
| Water | do | do | Aug. 15 | Aug. 1 | July 15 | Sept. 15 | |
| Cucumber | | | Oct. 15 | Oct. 1 | Sept. 15 | | |
| Dandelion | Dec. 1 | Nov. 1 | | | | June 1 | |
| Dasheen [1] | | | July 15 | July 1 | June 15 | Sept. 1 | Aug. 1 |
| Eggplant [1] | Sept. 1 | | Nov. 1 | Oct. 15 | Oct. 1 | July 1 | July 1 |
| Endive | Nov. 1 | Nov. 1 | Oct. 1 | Sept. 15 | Aug. 1 | | |
| Florence fennel | | | | | | | |
| Garlic [2] | | do | | Oct. 1 | Sept. 1 | July 1 | Do. |
| Horseradish [1] | | | | | | do | June 15 |
| Jerusalem artichoke | Nov. 1 | Nov. 1 | Nov. 1 | Oct. 1 | Sept. 15 | June 1 | May 15 |
| Kale | do | Oct. 1 | Sept. 1 | Aug. 15 | July 15 | July 15 | July 1 |
| Kohlrabi | | do | July 15 | July 1 | Aug. 1 | Aug. 1 | July 15 |
| Leek | Dec. 1 | Nov. 1 | Oct. 1 | Sept. 1 | Sept. 1 | | |
| Lettuce | Nov. 15 | do | Oct. 15 | Oct. 1 | Sept. 1 | Sept. 1 | Aug. 15 |
| Martynia | | | | | | | |
| Muskmelon [2] | Dec. 1 | Nov. 15 | Nov. 1 | Oct. 15 | Oct. 1 | | |
| Mustard | Oct. 1 | Sept. 15 | July 15 | July 1 | June 15 | | |
| Okra | | | | | | | |

# THE FARM GARDEN

| | | | | | | |
|---|---|---|---|---|---|---|
| Onion: | | | | | | |
| Plants | Dec. 15 | | | | June 1 | May 15. |
| Seed | Dec. 1 | | Oct. 15 | do | June 1 | Do. |
| Sets | Dec. 15 | | July 15 | July 1 | July 15 | July 1. |
| Parsley | Dec. 1 | | Nov. 1 | Sept. 1 | June 15 | Do. |
| Parsley, turnip-rooted | do | | do | do | | |
| Parsnip | do | | June 15 | June 1 | Aug. 15 | Aug. 15. |
| Peas | Nov. 1 | | Sept. 1 | Aug. 15 | June 1 | June 1. |
| Peppers[1] | Sept. 15 | | July 15 | July 1 | do | |
| Physalis | Sept. 1 | | Aug. 15 | July 15 | | |
| Poke[1] | do | | | | July 1 | June 15. |
| Potato | Sept. 15 | | Aug. 15 | Aug. 1 | do | Do. |
| Pumpkin | do | | do | do | Sept. 1 | Aug. 15. |
| Radish | Dec. 1 | | Oct. 15 | Oct. 1 | Nov. 1 | Nov. 1. |
| Rhubarb[1] | | | | Nov. 1 | June 15 | June 1. |
| Rutabagas | Nov. 1 | | Nov. 1 | June 1 | | |
| Salsify | Dec. 1 | | | | | |
| Shallots | do | | Oct. 1 | Oct. 1 | July 15 | July 15. |
| Sorrel | do | | Oct. 15 | do | Aug. 1 | Aug. 1. |
| Spinach | Nov. 1 | | Aug. 1 | July 15 | June 15 | |
| Spinach, New Zealand | Oct. 1 | | | | | |
| Squash: | | | | | | |
| Summer | Oct. 1 | Sept. 1 | Aug. 15 | Aug. 1 | July 15 | June 15. |
| Winter | | | July 15 | July 1 | June 15 | Do. |
| Sweetpotato[1],[2] | | | | | | |
| Tomato[1] | Oct. 1 | Sept. 1 | Aug. 15 | July 15 | July 1 | July 15. |
| Turnip greens | Nov. 15 | Nov. 1 | Oct. 15 | Oct. 1 | June 15 | July 1. |
| Turnips | do | do | do | Sept. 1 | Aug. 1 | |
| Watermelon[2] | | | | | July 15 | |

[1] Plants.  [2] Spring planting only.

Table 3 gives in general the proper depth of planting for the various vegetable seeds as well as the quantity of seeds or number of plants required for 100 feet of row and the distance apart that plants should be spaced. Special planting suggestions will be found under the discussion of cultural hints for the various garden crops.

TABLE 3.—*Quantity of seeds and number of plants required for 100 feet of row, depths of planting, and distances apart for rows and plants*

| Crop | Required for 100 feet of row | | Depth for planting seed | Distance apart | | |
|---|---|---|---|---|---|---|
| | | | | Rows | | Plants in the row |
| | Seed | Plants | | Horse cultivation | Hand cultivation | |
| | | | *Inches* | *Feet* | | |
| Asparagus | 1 ounce | 75 | 1 -1½ | 4 -5 | 1½ to 2 feet | 18 inches. |
| Beans: | | | | | | |
| Lima, bush | 1 pint | | 1 -1½ | 2½-3 | 2 feet | 3 to 4 inches. |
| Lima, pole | do | | 1 -1½ | 3 -4 | 3 feet | 3 to 4 feet. |
| Snap, bush | do | | 1 -1½ | 2½-3 | 2 feet | 3 to 4 inches. |
| Snap, pole | ½ pint | | 1 -1½ | 3 -4 | do | 3 feet. |
| Beet | 2 ounces | | 1 | 2 -2½ | 14 to 16 inches | 2 to 3 inches. |
| Broccoli: | | | | | | |
| Heading | 1 packet | 50- 75 | ½ | 2½-3 | 2 to 2½ feet | 14 to 24 inches. |
| Sprouting | do | 50- 75 | ½ | 2½-3 | do | Do. |
| Brussels sprouts | do | 50- 75 | ½ | 2½-3 | do | Do. |
| Cabbage | do | 50- 75 | ½ | 2½-3 | do | Do. |
| Cabbage, Chinese | do | | ½ | 2 -2½ | 18 to 24 inches | 8 to 12 inches. |
| Cardoon | do | 35 | ½ | 3 | 3 feet | 3 feet. |
| Carrot | do | | ½ | 2 -2½ | 14 to 16 inches | 2 to 3 inches. |
| Cauliflower | do | 50- 75 | ½ | 2½-3 | 2 to 2½ feet | 14 to 24 inches. |
| Celeriac | do | 200-250 | ⅛ | 2½-3 | 18 to 24 inches | 4 to 6 inches. |
| Celery | do | 200-250 | ⅛ | 2½-3 | do | Do. |
| Chard | 2 ounces | | 1 | 2 -2½ | do | 6 inches. |
| Chervil | 1 packet | | ½ | 2 -2½ | 14 to 16 inches | 2 to 3 inches. |
| Chicory, witloof | do | | ½ | 2 -2½ | 18 to 24 inches | 6 to 8 inches. |
| Chives | do | | ½ | 2½-3 | 14 to 16 inches | In clusters. |
| Collards | do | | ½ | 3 -3½ | 18 to 24 inches | 18 to 24 inches. |
| Corn salad | do | | ½ | 2½-3 | 14 to 16 inches | 1 foot. |
| Corn, sweet | ¼ pint | | 2 | 3 -3½ | 2 to 3 feet | Drills, 14 to 16 inches; hills, 2½ to 3 feet. |
| Cress: | | | | | | |
| Upland | 1 packet | | ⅛- ¼ | 2 -2½ | 14 to 16 inches | 2 to 3 inches. |
| Water | do | | ⅛- ¼ | 2 -2½ | 18 to 24 inches | 4 to 6 inches. |
| Cucumber | do | | 1 | 6 -7 | 6 to 7 feet | Drills, 3 feet; hills, 6 feet. |
| Dandelion | do | | ½ | 2½-3 | 14 to 16 inches | 8 to 12 inches. |
| Dasheen | ½ peck | 50 | 2 -3 | 3½-4 | 3½ to 4 feet | 2 feet. |
| Eggplant | 1 packet | 50 | ½ | 3 | 2 to 2½ feet | 3 feet. |
| Endive | do | | ½ | 2½-3 | 18 to 24 inches | 12 inches. |
| Florence fennel | do | | ½ | 2½-3 | do | 4 to 6 inches. |
| Garlic | 1 pound | | 1 -2 | 2½-3 | 14 to 16 inches | 2 to 3 inches. |
| Horseradish | Cuttings | 50- 75 | 2 | 3 -4 | 2 to 2½ feet | 18 to 24 inches. |
| Jerusalem artichoke | 1 to 2 quarts | 25- 35 | 2 -3 | 3 -4 | 2 to 3 feet | 2 to 3 feet. |
| Kale | 1 packet | | ½ | 2½-3 | 18 to 24 inches | 12 to 15 inches. |
| Kohlrabi | do | | ½ | 2½-3 | 14 to 16 inches | 5 to 6 inches. |
| Leek | do | | ½-1 | 2½-3 | do | 2 to 3 inches. |
| Lettuce | do | 100 | ½ | 2½-3 | do | 15 inches. |
| Martynia | do | | 1 | 3 -4 | 2½ to 3 feet | 2 feet. |
| Muskmelon | do | | 1 | 6 -7 | 6 to 7 feet | Hills, 6 feet. |
| Mustard | do | | ½ | 2½-3 | 14 to 16 inches | 12 inches. |
| Okra | 2 ounces | | 1 -1½ | 3 -3½ | 3 to 3½ feet | 2 feet. |
| Onion: | | | | | | |
| Plants | | 400 | 1 -2 | 2 -2½ | 14 to 16 inches | 2 to 3 inches. |
| Seed | 1 packet | | ½-1 | 2 -2½ | do | Do. |
| Sets | 1 quart | | 1 -2 | 2 -2½ | do | Do. |
| Parsley | 1 packet | | ⅛ | 2 -2½ | do | 4 to 6 inches. |
| Parsley, turnip-rooted. | do | | ⅛- ¼ | 2 -2½ | do | 2 to 3 inches. |
| Parsnip | do | | ½ | 2 -2½ | 18 to 24 inches | Do. |
| Peas | 1 pint | | 2 -3 | 2 -4 | 1½ to 3 feet | 1 inch. |
| Peppers | 1 packet | 50- 70 | ½ | 3 -4 | 2 to 3 feet | 18 to 24 inches. |
| Physalis | do | | ½ | 2 -2½ | 1½ to 2 feet | 12 to 18 inches. |
| Poke | do | 25- 40 | ½-1 | 3 -3½ | 3 to 3½ feet | 3 feet. |
| Potato | 5 to 6 pounds | | 4 | 2½-3 | 2 to 2½ feet | 10 to 18 inches. |
| Pumpkin | 1 ounce | | 1 -2 | 5 -8 | 5 to 8 feet | 3 to 4 feet. |

TABLE 3.—*Quantity of seeds and number of plants required for 100 feet of row, depths of planting, and distances apart for rows and plants*—Continued

| Crop | Required for 100 feet of row | | Depth for planting seed | Distance apart | | |
|---|---|---|---|---|---|---|
| | | | | Rows | | |
| | Seed | Plants | | Horse cultivation | Hand cultivation | Plants in the row |
| | | | *Inches* | *Feet* | | |
| Radish | 1 ounce | | ½ | 2 -2½ | 14 to 16 inches | 1 inch. |
| Rhubarb | | 25- 35 | | 3 -4 | 3 to 4 feet | 3 to 4 feet. |
| Salsify | 1 ounce | | ½ | 2 -2½ | 18 to 24 inches | 2 to 3 inches. |
| Shallots | 1 pound (cloves) | | 1 -2 | 2 -2½ | 14 to 16 inches | Do. |
| Sorrel | 1 packet | | ½ | 2 -2½ | 18 to 24 inches | 5 to 8 inches. |
| Spinach | 1 ounce | | ½ | 2 -2½ | 14 to 16 inches | 3 to 6 inches. |
| Spinach, New Zealand | do | | 1 -1½ | 3 -3½ | 3 feet | 18 inches. |
| Squash: | | | | | | |
| Bush | ½ ounce | | 1 -2 | 4 -5 | 4 to 5 feet | Drills, 15 to 18 inches; hills, 4 feet. |
| Vine | 1 ounce | | 1 -2 | 8 -12 | 8 to 12 feet | Drills, 2 to 3 feet; hills, 4 feet. |
| Sweetpotato | 5 pounds | [1] 75 | 2 -3 | 3 -3½ | 3 to 3½ feet | 12 to 14 inches. |
| Tomato | 1 packet | 35- 50 | ½ | 3 -4 | 2 to 3 feet | 1½ to 3 feet. |
| Turnip greens | do | | ¼- ½ | 2 -2½ | 14 to 16 inches | 2 to 3 inches. |
| Turnips and rutabagas | ½ ounce | | ¼- ½ | 2 -2½ | do | Do. |
| Watermelon | 1 ounce | | 1 -2 | 8 -10 | 8 to 10 feet | Drills, 2 to 3 feet; hills, 8 feet. |

[1] Slips.

## SUCCESSION OF CROPS

All garden space should be kept fully occupied throughout the growing season. In the South this means the greater part of the year; in fact, throughout the South Atlantic and Gulf coast regions it is possible to have certain vegetables growing in the garden every month of the year.

In arranging the garden all early maturing crops may properly be grouped so that after their removal the ground will be available as a unit for planting later crops. As soon as one crop is removed another should take its place. It is not desirable, however, to follow a crop with another of its kind, but with some unrelated crop. For example, early peas or beans can very properly be followed by late cabbage, celery, carrots, or beets; early corn or potatoes can be followed by fall turnips or spinach. It is not always necessary to wait until the early crop is entirely removed, but a later crop may be planted between the rows of the early crop; for example, sweet corn may be planted between the rows of early potatoes. Late cabbage is frequently planted between potato rows. Crops that are attacked by the same diseases should not follow each other.

In the extreme North, where the season is relatively short, there is very little opportunity for succession cropping; therefore plenty of land should be provided to accommodate the desired range of crops.

## THE LATE SUMMER AND FALL GARDEN

Farmers the country over would be justified in paying more attention to their late summer and fall gardens. Second and third plantings of crops adapted to growing late in the season not only provide a supply of fresh vegetables for the latter part of the season but give better products for canning and storing. This is particularly true of beans, beets, carrots, and celery. Late-grown beans are especially suitable for canning, while the root crops and celery when matured late in the season are crisp and tender and of better quality for having escaped the summer's heat. In parts of the South the autumn garden is really of as great importance as the early one.

## CULTIVATION

Frequent shallow cultivation should be given most garden crops, mainly to keep the garden free from weeds and the surface soil loose and mellow. Weeds draw heavily on the moisture supply and the plant food of the soil; therefore the best time to destroy weeds is just after they start. If the crops are cultivated once a week, especially during the early part of the season, weeds will be controlled, and the crops will get the benefit of the moisture and soil fertility. Under no circumstances should the land be cultivated when wet, but in sections having natural rainfall the garden should be gone over with the cultivator as soon as it is dry enough after a rain to break the crust and thus prevent the baking of the surface soil. If the work is done properly and at regular intervals there will be little difficulty in controlling weeds and keeping the garden crops growing.

FIGURE 10.—A 5-shovel cultivator with attachments, adapted for garden cultivation

A 1-horse, 5-shovel cultivator with various attachments, of the type shown in Figure 10, is suited for garden cultivation. In all cases the cultivator should be fitted with a lever or some device to regulate its width. Cultivators that stir the soil deeply should not, under most circumstances, be used in the garden, except where some crops, such as potatoes, require the soil to be worked into a ridge about the plants. A sweep should not be used, except possibly in the middles between the rows. The larger crops in the garden should be cultivated with horse-drawn tools and with a minimum of hand labor. The smaller crops, such as carrots, beets, and lettuce, if planted in rows too close for horse cultivation, may be worked with a hand cultivator of the type shown in Figure 11. This implement is fitted with a variety of attachments, enabling the gardener to do many kinds of work.

Hand tools needed in the garden are mainly a hoe, a steel rake, a spade or a spading fork, a planting trowel, a watering can, and a garden line for laying off the rows. It is not necessary to have a large investment in tools. Generally the implements used for other purposes on the farm are adaptable for work in the garden.

## IRRIGATION

Throughout that portion of the country where rains occur during the growing season it should not be necessary to irrigate in order to produce the ordinary garden crops. In arid regions where irrigation must be depended upon for the production of crops, the system best adapted for use in that particular locality should be employed in the garden. Wherever irrigation is practiced the water should not be applied until needed, and then the soil should be thoroughly soaked. After irrigation the land should be cultivated as soon as the surface becomes sufficiently dry, and no more water should be applied until the plants begin to show the need of additional moisture. Constant or excessive watering is very detrimental in every case. Apply the water at any time of the day that is most convenient and when the plants require it.

Overhead or sprinkler irrigation is now used extensively in commercial market gardens, especially in sections where the natural rainfall is insufficient at certain periods of the growing season. This system is also suited for use in the home garden if there is an adequate supply of water under pressure. Manufacturers of overhead or sprinkler equipment provide temporary lines of sprinkler pipe which are connected by unions and may be put together or taken apart very quickly. A hose connects the pipe with the water system. These pipes may be supported on stakes, on blocks of wood, or on crates or boxes placed in a row through the garden.[4]

FIGURE 11.—A small hand cultivator, a desirable addition to the garden equipment

## PAPER MULCH

Gardening under paper, or the use of paper as a mulch, has been advocated as a means of eliminating cultivation, controlling weeds, increasing yields, conserving moisture, and raising the temperature of the soil. Under many conditions the use of paper mulch has proved to be advantageous and largely increased yields have been obtained. In some instances the advantages have not justified the expense and labor involved in applying the paper. For the home gardener, however, the chief interest in mulch paper lies in the fact that it reduces the necessity for cultivation during hot weather. The use of paper will control weeds, although a certain amount of hand weeding may be needed around individual plants or between

---

[4] For further information on overhead irrigation, see Farmers' Bulletin 1529, Spray Irrigation in the Eastern States.

the strips of paper. Paper mulch has hastened the maturity and increased the yields of certain garden crops, particularly those requiring a long season, such as sweetpotatoes, peppers, eggplant, and tomatoes, especially in the more northern States.

Paper mulch as used in home gardens has given most general satisfaction when laid in strips held with a continuous ridge of soil over the depressed edges. Following the laying of the paper over the moist garden soil, the transplants such as tomatoes, cauliflower, and peppers are set at the desired intervals through openings made in the paper with a sharp stick or dibble. Crops such as potatoes, corn, beans, and melons may be seeded through similar openings. The use of mulch paper with small-seeded drill crops requires special methods which vary with the conditions.

While the heavier (type B) mulch papers have proved most suitable for garden use, the lighter (type A) papers have sometimes proved serviceable, particularly on light soils or in regions of reduced rainfall. The cost of the heavier paper required for a plot 50 by 50 feet when used in the manner above described is about $7 and that of the lighter paper about $3.50.

### INSECTS AND DISEASES

The insects and diseases that infest garden crops are so numerous that it would be impracticable even to mention them all in a bulletin of this character. There are certain control measures, however, that will often accomplish a great amount of good. In the autumn after the crops have been harvested, or as fast as any crop is disposed of, all refuse that remains should be gathered and burned. Some of the garden insects and disease-producing organisms winter in the remains of garden crops and in the trash and weeds around the garden. By burning such material many of these insects and disease organisms are destroyed.

There are two main classes of insects to be dealt with. The chewing or biting insects may for the most part be controlled by the use of stomach poisons, such as lead arsenate or Paris green, or by hand collection or other special methods. The sucking insects, especially the plant lice, must be controlled by contact poisons, such as nicotine or pyrethrum.

For the diseases of vegetables, numerous methods of control are available. Sometimes a single method is effective, but more often several measures must be combined to secure the best results. An illustration of the former is the use of varieties resistant to disease. An example of the latter is the combination of rotation of crops, seed treatment, and spraying for the control of anthracnose of cucurbits.

Among the most important disease-control measures are crop rotation, soil treatment, the use of disease-free seed and plants, seed treatment with fungicides, the use of disease-resistant varieties, spraying and dusting with fungicides, and the eradication of wild host plants on which certain diseases overwinter.[5]

---

[5] For details of these control methods see Farmers' Bulletin 1371, Diseases and Insects of Garden Vegetables, and Yearbook Separate 929, Diseases and Pests of Fruits and Vegetables.

## CANNING AND STORING VEGETABLES AT HOME

In sections of the country where a constant supply of fresh vegetables can not be obtained from the garden throughout the year, it is important that the season for their use be extended by means of canning and storage. Nonacid vegetables, such as asparagus, beans, corn, peas, beets, and spinach, should be canned under steam pressure rather than by the hot-water process. Tomatoes, being an acid vegetable, may be safely canned by the boiling-water process. Pressure cookers are now standard equipment in many homes and may be used for the canning of vegetables. It is important, however, that the pressure cooker be equipped with thermometer, pressure gauge, and safety valve for proper control. There are also on the market satisfactory hand machines for sealing tin cans, making it possible to apply factory methods in the canning of vegetables in the home.[6]

The home storage of vegetables is, perhaps, of greater importance than canning because of its adaptation to all that portion of the country where freezing temperatures prevail during the winter months. There are at least 10 important vegetables that can be stored for winter use, the success attending their storage depending largely on the way the work is handled. Certain vegetables, like cabbage, turnips, beets, carrots, and celery, may be stored in pits in the open ground; potatoes, sweetpotatoes, and onions are stored to best advantage in cellars or specially designed storage houses. Temperature, moisture control, and ventilation are the main points involved in the successful home storage of vegetables.[7]

The root crops, including beets, carrots, winter radishes, and turnips, also such crops as collards, kale, and spinach, may remain where they are grown throughout the late fall and early winter in nearly all parts of the South. These crops, however, will start a new growth as soon as the weather begins to get warm in the late winter and will produce seed stalks, after which they are unfit for the table. In sections of the South where temperature conditions make it impossible to store vegetables for off-season use, canning and drying should be substituted.

## CULTURE OF SPECIFIC GARDEN CROPS

### PERENNIAL VEGETABLES

Perennial vegetables, especially asparagus, horseradish, and rhubarb, are among the most valuable garden products. They occupy comparatively little space and when once planted continue to yield for a number of years. It is usually best to locate these perennials along one side of the garden where they do not interfere with work on the annual plants. Unfortunately, these three important perennials are not adapted to culture in all sections and can not be grown in parts of the lower South. Because of their desirability, the perennials should be included in every garden where space and adaptability permit their culture.

---

[6] Farmers' Bulletin 1471, Canning Fruits and Vegetables at Home, gives information on proper methods of canning.
[7] Farmers' Bulletin 879, Home Storage of Vegetables, gives information relative to storage structures and methods of caring for vegetables in storage.

## ASPARAGUS

Asparagus is wholesome and in many sections is among the earliest of the spring vegetables. An area about 20 feet square, or a row 50 to 75 feet long, will supply plenty of asparagus for a family of five or six persons, provided the soil is well enriched and the plants are given good attention.

Asparagus does best in locations having winters sufficiently cold to freeze the ground to a depth of at least a few inches, but it is not adapted to all portions of the lower South. In many southern locations the plants make a weak growth, producing small shoots. Elevation has some effect, but in general the latitude of south-central Georgia is about the southern limit of profitable culture.

The crop can be grown on almost any well-drained, fertile soil, and there is little possibility of having the land too rich, especially through the use of manure. As an asparagus planting will last for many years, it should be located where it will interfere as little as possible with other gardening operations.

Since asparagus roots go deep for their supply of moisture and plant food, the land should be loosened far down either by subsoil plowing or deep spading before planting. It is a good plan to throw the topsoil aside and spade manure, leaf mold, rotted leaves, or peat into the subsoil to a depth of 14 to 16 inches. From 5 to 10 pounds of a complete fertilizer should also be mixed into each 75-foot row or 20-foot bed.

FIGURE 12.—Asparagus crowns or plants being set in a trench

When ready for planting, the bottom of the trench should be about 6 inches below the natural level of the soil. (Fig. 12.) After the crowns are set and covered to a depth of an inch or two, the soil should be gradually worked into the trench around the plants during the first season. When set in beds, asparagus plants should be at least 1½ feet apart each way; when set in rows, they should be about 18 inches apart, with the rows from 4 to 5 feet apart.

Asparagus plants or crowns are grown from seed. The use of 1-year-old plants only is recommended. These should have a root spread of at least 15 inches, and larger ones are better. The home gardener will usually find it best to purchase his plants from some grower who has a good strain of a recognized variety. Mary Washington is a good variety that has the added merit of being rust resistant. In procuring asparagus crowns it is always well to be sure that they have not been allowed to dry out.

Clean cultivation encourages vigorous growth. Weeds and grass are usually responsible for unsatisfactory results with asparagus, and it behooves the gardener to keep his asparagus clean from the start. In the large farm garden with long rows most of the work can be done with a horse-drawn cultivator, but in the small garden, where the rows are short, or the asparagus is planted in beds, handwork must be resorted to.

White asparagus is produced by mounding the rows or hills with earth to keep light away from the young spears. Hilling is begun during the early spring and continued throughout the cutting season as needed, but in most cases, especially on light-textured soils, the initial hilling should be sufficient. On heavier soils the earth must be added more slowly. At the end of the cutting season these ridges are leveled down.

It is well to make an annual application of manure to asparagus. A liberal dressing of a high-grade complete fertilizer, 6 to 8 pounds to a 75-foot row, once each year, is also necessary. Both manure and fertilizer should be used at the end of the cutting season.

No shoots should be removed the year the plants are set in the permanent bed, and the period of cutting should be short the year after setting. During the cutting season in subsequent years all shoots should be removed. About July 1 to 10 cutting should cease and the tops should be allowed to grow. In the autumn, when dead, they can be removed and burned.

Asparagus rust and asparagus beetles are the chief enemies of asparagus. Directions for their control are given in Farmers' Bulletin 1371, Diseases and Insects of Garden Vegetables.[8]

### HORSERADISH

Horseradish is adapted for growing in the north-temperate regions of the United States, but it is not suited for planting in the South except possibly in the high altitudes. Grated horseradish is a very desirable condiment, always best when fresh. A few plants in an out-of-the-way place in the garden, such as a corner, will supply enough for the family.

Any good soil, except possibly the lightest sands and heaviest clays, will grow horseradish, but it does best on a deep, rich, moist loam that is well supplied with organic matter. A shallow soil should be avoided, as it produces rough, prongy roots. Manure should be mixed with the soil a few months before the plants or cuttings are set. Some fertilizer may be used at the time of planting and more during each subsequent season. A top-dressing of manure each spring is advisable, but a good, deep soil in an old garden will usually grow good horseradish without heavy manuring or fertilization.

Horseradish seldom forms seed; it is propagated either by using crowns or by root cuttings. In propagating by crowns, a portion of an old plant consisting of a piece of root and crown buds is merely lifted and placed in the new location. Root cuttings are pieces of older roots 6 to 8 inches long and of the thickness of a lead pencil. These may be saved when preparing the larger roots for grating, or they may be purchased from seedsmen. A trench 4 or 5 inches deep is opened with a hoe and the root cuttings placed at an angle with their tops near the surface of the ground. Each cutting will sprout in several places, and after they are well established the soil should be carefully removed by hand from around the cuttings. All but one good cluster of leaves near the top of each cutting should be removed. The soil should then be replaced. These plants usually

---

[8] Additional information on asparagus culture is given in Farmers' Bulletins 1242, Permanent Fruit and Vegetable Gardens, and 1646, Asparagus Culture.

make good roots the first year. As a rule the plants in the home garden are allowed to grow from year to year, and portions of the roots are removed as needed. Pieces of roots and crowns remaining in the soil are usually sufficient to reestablish the plants.

Horseradish is prepared by cleaning and grating the roots directly into white wine vinegar or distilled vinegar of 4½ to 5 per cent acid content. Bottled and sealed immediately, it keeps for a few weeks. Dried, ground, and bottled, it keeps for some time, but this product is not as good as when the horseradish is grated fresh and mixed with vinegar. Cider vinegar should not be used, as it causes the horseradish to turn dark.

### POKE

Poke, also known as scoke and garget, is grown and used to some extent as an early spring vegetable. The plant is commonly found growing wild along fences and around farmyards and in other places where rich, moist soil is to be found. Poke is a common carrier of the mosaic disease, and it should not be grown with crops susceptible to this disease.

Poke is propagated by taking portions from the crowns of the plant and setting these in a new location. The culture of poke is similar to that of asparagus. Poke must have a fertile soil; but given that, no additional fertilization is needed. Like horseradish, poke may be planted along one side of the garden where it can remain for years. New plants soon arise from the old, and a few crowns spaced 2 to 3 feet apart soon occupy as much space as the average gardener cares to give it.

The young shoots that come up first in spring are used for food. They are taken just as they come through the loose earth and while they are still white and tender. Mulching with leaves or straw will aid in keeping the shoots white and tender. They are cut in the same way as asparagus, but care should be taken to avoid taking any portion of the root, as it contains a poisonous alkaloid. Poke is cooked, seasoned, and eaten in the same way as asparagus or as greens.

### RHUBARB

Rhubarb thrives best in regions having cool moist summers and winters sufficiently cold to freeze the ground to a depth of several inches. It is not adapted to most portions of the South, but in certain regions of higher elevation it does fairly well. Rhubarb, like asparagus, is a perennial, and a few hills along the garden fence will supply all that a family can use. In sections where it thrives, rhubarb should be in the garden, for it comes early in the spring and has fine dietetic qualities.

Any deep, well-drained, fertile soil is suitable for rhubarb. It should be spaded or plowed to a depth of 12 to 16 inches, and rotted manure, leaf mold, decayed hardwood leaves, sods, or some other form of organic matter should be mixed with it. The methods of soil preparation suggested for asparagus are suitable for rhubarb; but as rhubarb is planted in hills 3 to 4 feet apart, it is usually sufficient to prepare each hill separately.

Rhubarb plants may be started from seed and transplanted, but seedlings vary from the parent plant. The usual method of starting the plants is to obtain pieces of crowns from established hills and set them in prepared hills. Cultivation is confined to the control of weeds. The planting should be top-dressed with a heavy application of manure in either early spring or late fall. Fresh horse manure applied over the hills during early spring greatly hastens growth or " forces " the plant.

If plenty of manure can be obtained, rhubarb needs little if any commercial fertilizer. However, a pound of complete commercial fertilizer high in nitrogen applied around each hill every year insures an abundant supply of plant food. In the absence of manure the plants can be mulched with green grass or weeds, and commercial fertilizer may be applied more liberally, but some manure is very desirable.

Seed stalks should be removed as soon as they form, because seed bearing greatly weakens the plant. No leaf stems should be harvested before the second year and but few until the third. Moreover, the harvest season must be largely confined to early spring as the plants should be allowed to grow undisturbed during summer. The hills should be divided and reset every seven or eight years. If not, they become too thick and produce only slender stems.

Only the leaf stem of the rhubarb is used as a vegetable. The leaves contain injurious materials such as oxalic acid, and in no case should they be used for food. They make excellent covers to protect tomato, cabbage, and other plants for the first day or two after setting.

### GREENS

Greens may be defined as the leaves and stems of young plants, such as spinach, which in their green state are boiled for food. The classification of greens in this bulletin is an arrangement of convenience, for plants such as collards are really greens also. The plants treated here as greens are hardy vegetables most of which are adapted to fall sowing and winter culture over the entire South and the more temperate portions of the North. Their culture may be extended over a wider area of the North by growing them with some protection, such as mulching or frames. Greens are especially valuable vegetables in that they are high in salts and vitamins.

### CARDOON

Cardoon is a large thistlelike plant (fig. 13) which is grown for its fleshy leaf stems. In the North the seeds are sown in early spring in a hotbed or coldframe and the plants transplanted later to the open ground. In the South the seed may be sown in the rows where the plants are to be grown. The plants should be placed about 3 feet apart each way in rich soil with plenty of moisture, but they do not thrive on poorly drained land. Toward autumn the leaves are drawn together and blanched by wrapping with paper, by slipping a draintile over each plant, or by other methods of excluding light. If intended for winter use, the leaves are not blanched in the garden, but the plants are lifted with considerable earth adhering to the roots and stored in a cellar or pit to blanch.

FIGURE 13.—Cardoon, a large thistlelike plant which is bleached for use

The leafstalks are boiled and served as a green or used in the making of soups and stews. Cardoon is usually somewhat bitter, and it has only a limited field of usefulness as a home garden crop.

### CHARD

Chard, or Swiss chard, is a type of beet that has been developed for its tops instead of its roots. The leaves are cooked and used as greens in very much the same way as spinach. The thickened leaf stems are sometimes cooked and used in much the same way as asparagus. One of the advantages of this vegetable is that crop after crop of the outer leaves may be harvested without injuring the plant. Only one planting is necessary, and a row 30 to 40 feet long will supply a family for the entire summer. Figure 14 shows the habit of growth of Swiss chard. Its culture is practically the same as that of beets, but the plants grow larger and should be thinned to at least 6 inches apart in the row. In common with beets, chard demands a rich mellow soil; and as it is sensitive to soil acidity, it is usually wise to use a little lime on the land before planting it. The seed clusters each contain several seeds, and fairly wide spacing will facilitate thinning.

FIGURE 14.—Swiss chard, excellent hot-weather greens

## DANDELION

The dandelion is hardy and adapted to much the same conditions as kale and mustard. It will grow on almost any garden soil. In the North the seeds are usually sown during early spring in rows about 18 inches apart and covered to a depth of about half an inch. The plants should be thinned to 8 to 12 inches apart in the rows and cultivated throughout the summer. (Fig. 15.) In the colder parts of the country it may be desirable to mulch slightly during the winter, using leaves, straw, or strawy manure. Early the following spring the plants will be ready for use as greens. In the South, the seed may be sown during the autumn, and the plants will be ready for use in the spring. Dandelion is greatly improved if blanched by being covered with paper or by having two boards set in the form of a letter A over the row. The blanching not only makes the leaves more tender but destroys part of the bitter taste.

FIGURE 15.—Dandelion, which under favorable conditions gives a heavy yield of greens

## KALE

Kale, or borecole, is hardy like spinach and lives over winter in latitudes as far north as northern Maryland and southern Pennsylvania and in other locations where similar winter conditions prevail. It is also resistant to heat and may be grown in summer, but its real merit is as cool-weather greens.

Kale is a member of the cabbage family, and the best garden varieties are low-growing, spreading plants with thick, more or less crinkled leaves. (Fig. 16.) Scotch Curled and Siberian are two of the best-known garden varieties.

In the home garden in the North kale may be seeded almost any time from early

FIGURE 16.—Kale, hardy and popular greens

spring until a few weeks before hard frost. In northern regions where it lives over winter the last sowing should be about six weeks before frost in order that the plants may become well established. In the South it may be seeded almost any time, but it has little to commend it during midsummer and is seldom sown to mature during this season. No other plant is so well adapted to fall sowing throughout a wide area both North and South or in regions characterized by winters of moderate severity. It may well follow green beans, potatoes, peas, or some other vegetable that has occupied the ground during the early season.

Almost any garden soil will grow good kale. When it follows in the same season another crop that has been fertilized, kale should need little if any additional plant food. It may be broadcast like turnips, particularly when seeded during the autumn; but for spring sowings, made at a time when weeds are troublesome, row seeding is advised. The seed should be covered lightly, usually by being raked in with a garden rake. Cultivation is limited to that necessary for the control of weeds.

Kale may be harvested either by cutting the entire plant or by taking the larger leaves while young. Old kale is liable to be tough and stringy. The culture of kale is easy, and the gardener is advised to pay more attention to this excellent green.

### MUSTARD

Almost any good soil will produce a crop of mustard. The basal leaves are used for greens; and as the plants require but a short time to reach the proper stage for use, frequent sowings should be made. Sow the seeds thickly in drills as early as possible in the spring, or for late use sow in September or October. The forms of Chinese or Japanese mustard, the leaves of which are often curled and frilled, are generally used. Mustard greens are cooked like spinach.

### SPINACH

Spinach is by far the most popular of the greens. It is a reasonably hardy cool-weather plant that withstands winter conditions throughout most portions of the South. In colder portions of the Southern States it may need some protection during the winter, for, like cabbage and other hardy crops, it is sometimes severely injured or even killed by low temperatures. In most portions of the North spinach is primarily an early spring and late fall crop, but in certain locations where summer temperatures are mild it may be grown continuously from early spring until late fall. It should be emphasized that the summer and winter culture of spinach is possible only where moderate temperatures prevail.

Spinach will grow on almost any type of well-drained, fertile soil where sufficient moisture is available. If possible a rich friable loam with an abundance of organic matter should be used. The home gardener will find spinach adapted to his land whether it be a heavy clay or a peat so long as it is well-drained and rich. Spinach is very sensitive to acid soil; if any doubt exists regarding the need of the soil for lime, it may be wise to apply a few pounds to the portion of the garden devoted to spinach, irrespective of the treatment given the remainder of the area.

The general application of both manure and fertilizer to the garden has been advised in an earlier portion of this bulletin. Spinach will profitably use additional supplies of both. A pound of rotted manure to each square foot and 3 to 4 pounds of commercial fertilizer to each 100 square feet of land is suggested as suitable rates of application for spinach in the home garden. Both manure and fertilizer should be applied broadcast and raked in before the spinach is sown.

In the North spinach may be sown as early in the spring as it is possible to prepare the ground. Two or three successive plantings at intervals of one week should be made until the approach of hot weather or about June 1, but these later plantings can not be expected to yield as heavily as the earlier ones. Plantings may again be started during the late summer and continue until about six weeks before frost. In sections having cool summers, plantings may be made in succession throughout the growing season or until a few weeks before frost. In the South the time of planting depends upon locality and season. In general it extends from early fall to late spring, but it is useless to attempt spinach culture in midsummer. The zone maps and tables give the approximate dates for sowing spinach in various parts of the country.

Bloomsdale Savoy, Prickly Seeded, and Victoria are desirable varieties. The first-named should not be used for the later sowings in the spring, because it shoots to seed readily in hot weather. Virginia Savoy is a most valuable variety for fall planting because of its superior hardiness and resistance to "blight," which may occur in the autumn, but it is not suitable for spring planting. Great care should be taken to obtain seed that is fresh and of good quality. For horse cultivation the rows should be not less than 24 inches apart, and when land is plentiful they may be 30 inches apart. For garden tractor, wheel hoe, or handwork the rows should be 12 to 18 inches apart. Spinach may be drilled by hand in furrows about 1 inch deep made with a hoe or other device and covered with fine earth not more than one-half inch deep, or it may be drilled with a seed drill, which distributes the seed more evenly than is ordinarily possible by hand. The use of the drill is advised. The plants should be thinned to 3 or 4 inches apart before they crowd in the row.

#### NEW ZEALAND SPINACH

New Zealand spinach is not related to common spinach. It is a large plant with thickish leaves and stems and grows with a branching, spreading habit to a height of 2 or more feet. It thrives in hot weather and is grown as a substitute at seasons when the ordinary spinach can not withstand the heat. New Zealand spinach thrives on soils suitable for common spinach. Because of the larger size of these plants they must be given more room. The rows should be at least 3 feet apart, with the plants about 2 feet apart in the rows. The seeds may be sown 1 to 1½ inches deep as soon as danger of frost is past. As some difficulty may be experienced in getting the seeds to germinate promptly, they should be soaked for one or two hours in water at 120° F. before planting. Successive harvests of the tips may be made from a single planting, since new leaves and branches are readily produced. Care must be taken not to remove too large a portion of the plant at one time lest later harvests suffer. New Zealand spinach is cooked the same way as common spinach.

### SORREL

Sorrel is not well known to the majority of gardeners, yet it is highly prized by many, especially for cooking with spinach to give it added flavor. It is a perennial plant that is usually started from seeds. It requires a rich, mellow, well-drained soil. Rows may be of any convenient width, and the plants should be thinned to about 8 inches apart in the rows. If the leaves alone are gathered and the plants are cultivated to prevent the growth of weeds, a planting should last three or four years. Broad-Leaved French is a well-known variety.

### TURNIP GREENS

Varieties of turnips usually grown for the roots are also planted especially for the greens. Strains of turnips especially suitable for greens are now available under different names. In some cases turnips are seeded thickly and thinned for use as greens, the rest being left to develop as a root crop. Turnip greens are especially adapted to winter and early spring culture in the South. The cultural methods employed are the same as those described under Turnip and Rutabaga (p. 47).

The Seven-Top turnip is also sown and allowed to grow until young succulent seed stalks are formed, these being cut and used as greens. These sprouts are sometimes erroneously called "brockley" or broccoli.

### SALAD CROPS

The group known as salad crops includes vegetables that are usually eaten raw with salt, vinegar, pepper, or salad oils, or with mayonnaise or other dressings. This classification is entirely one of convenience, as other vegetables not included in this group are also used in the same way. Some members of this class are sometimes cooked and used as greens.

Lettuce and celery far outweigh all the other plants of this group in popularity. Practically every garden includes a bed or a few rows of lettuce, and it would be more generally grown if gardeners fully appreciated its possibilities.

### CELERY

Like most other vegetables, celery can be grown in home gardens in practically all parts of the country at some time during the year. It is a cool-weather crop and adapted to winter culture in the lower South. In the upper South and in the North it may be grown either as an early spring or as a late fall crop. Farther north in certain favored locations it can be grown throughout the summer.

Rich, moist, but well-drained, deeply prepared, mellow soil is essential for celery. Soil varying from sand to clay loam and to peat may be used as long as these requirements are met. Unless the ground is very fertile, plenty of well-rotted barnyard manure, supplemented by liberal applications of commercial fertilizer, is necessary. For a 100-foot row of celery, four or five wheelbarrow loads of manure and 5 pounds of a high-grade complete fertilizer thoroughly mixed with the soil is none too much. The celery row should be prepared a week or two before the plants are set.

The most common mistake with celery is failure to allow enough time for growing the plants. It requires about 10 weeks to grow good celery plants such as those shown in Figure 17. For the early crop in the North, which is set outdoors as soon as frosts are over, or about April 15 in the latitude of Indianapolis, Ind., the seeds must be sown in the hotbed or greenhouse about February 1. For the late crop in the same latitude, which is set about July 1, the plants must be started about April 15. The zone tables and maps indicate the planting dates for the various regions. Celery seed is small and germinates slowly. A good method is to place the seeds in a muslin bag and to soak them overnight, after which they are mixed with dry sand and distributed in shallow trenches in the seed flats or seed bed and covered with leaf mold or similar material to a depth of not more than one-eighth inch. The bed should be kept from drying out by covering with burlap sacks which are kept moist, or by similar means. Celery plants are very delicate and must be kept free from weeds. They are made more stocky by transplanting once before they are set in the garden, but this practice retards their growth. When they are to be transplanted before setting in the garden, the rows in the seed box or seed bed may be only a few inches apart; but if they are to remain in the box until transplanted to the garden, the plants should be about 2 inches apart each way. In beds, the rows should be 10 to 12 inches apart, with the seedlings 1 to 1½ inches apart in the row.

Celery may be set in single or double rows about 4 feet apart or in a bed. In single rows the plants are spaced about 6 inches apart; in double rows the spacing is the same, but two rows are placed side by side about 1 foot apart. In bed culture the plants may be set 1 foot apart each way. Row

FIGURE 17.—Two celery plants: Left, transplanted once before time for setting in the field; right, not transplanted from original seed bed

culture is usually best, especially when the celery is to be banked with earth. Set celery on a cool or cloudy day, if possible; and if the soil is at all dry, set the plants in place, cover the roots lightly, water, and then place more soil around them. If the plants are large, it is best to pinch off the outer leaves 3 or 4 inches from the base before setting. In bright weather it is also well to shade the plants for a day or two after setting. Small branches bearing green leaves, stuck in the ground, protect the plants from intense sun without excluding air. As soon as the plants attain some size the leaves should be drawn together and the soil gradually worked around the plants to keep them upright. Care must be taken to avoid getting soil into the hearts of the plants. Early celery is blanched with boards, paper, draintiles, or other devices for excluding the light. In addition to these means, late celery may be blanched also by banking with earth or by storing in the dark. Banking celery with soil in warm weather causes it to decay.

Late celery may be kept for early winter use by banking with earth and covering the tops with leaves or straw to keep them from freezing, or it may be dug and stored in a cellar or a coldframe, with the roots well embedded in moist soil. While in storage it must be kept as cool as possible without freezing.[9]

### WITLOOF CHICORY

Witloof chicory, sometimes called French endive, is grown for both roots and tops. It is a hardy plant that is not especially sensitive to heat or cold, but it does need a deep, rich, loamy soil without too much organic matter. The tops are harvested while young and boiled and eaten like spinach. It is necessary when boiling chicory to change the water once or twice to remove the bitterness. The roots are lifted in autumn and placed in a box or bed of moist soil in a warm cellar for forcing. They must be covered with a foot or two of manure, or a few inches of sand. Under this covering the leaves form in a solid head which is known on the market as witloof. These blanched leaves may be used as a raw salad or cooked and eaten like spinach or chard.

The culture of chicory is simple. The seeds are sown during spring or early summer in drills about 18 inches apart and the plants thinned to 6 or 8 inches apart in the rows. If sown too early the plants shoot to seed and are worthless for forcing. The kind known as witloof is most generally used.

### CORN SALAD

Corn salad is also known as lamb's-lettuce and fetticus. The seed is sown during the early spring in drills and the plants cultivated the same as for lettuce or mustard. For an extra-early crop the seed may be planted during the autumn and the plants covered lightly during the winter. In the Southern States the covering is not necessary, and the plants are ready for use during February and March. The leaves are frequently used in their natural green state, but they may be blanched by covering the rows with anything that will exclude the light. Corn salad is used as a salad in place of lettuce, or mixed with lettuce or water cress. Its flavor is very mild, and it is improved by mixing with some other salad plant. It is also boiled with mustard for greens.

### ENDIVE

Endive closely resembles lettuce in its requirements and habits of growth, except that it is not so sensitive to heat. It may be substituted for lettuce when the culture of lettuce is impracticable. In the South it is mainly a winter crop. In the North it is grown during the spring, summer, and autumn and is also forced during the winter. Endive is often known on the markets as escarolle. Broad-Leaved Batavian is a good sort.

The time of seeding is given in Tables 1 and 2 and depends upon the location. Sow the seeds thinly; and when the plants are established, thin to the same distance as for lettuce, or about 1 foot apart in the rows. When the plants are large and well-formed, draw the leaves together and tie so the heart will blanch. For winter use the

---

[9] For additional information on celery, see Farmers' Bulletin 1269, Celery Growing.

plants should be lifted with a ball of earth, placed in a cellar or coldframe where they will not freeze, and tied and blanched as needed.

Endive is used in the same way as lettuce. Its agreeable flavor makes it a most excellent addition to the list of vegetables. Figure 18 shows the appearance and character of endive.

### LETTUCE

Lettuce should be found in every home garden. It is a cool-weather crop, being as sensitive to heat as any vegetable grown. In the South lettuce culture is confined to late fall, winter, and spring. In colder portions of the South lettuce may not live through the winter, especially during seasons of low temperature. In the North lettuce culture is practically limited to the spring and autumn, as both winter and summer are too severe for it. In some favored locations, such as areas of high altitude or in far-northern latitudes, lettuce grows to perfection during the summer. In general, zones

FIGURE 18.—Broad-Leaved Batavian and Moss-Curled varieties of endive. The former is often called escarolle

A, B, and C shown in Figure 6 are adapted to fall, winter, and spring culture, and zones D, E, F, and G to spring and autumn culture. Frequent complaints from gardeners regarding poor results obtained with lettuce have been traced almost invariably to failure to realize its limitations, resulting in planting at the wrong season.

Any rich soil is adapted to lettuce. The plant is sensitive to lack of lime, and if the soil is strongly acid a few pounds of lime should be applied. A commercial fertilizer with a heavy proportion of phosphorus will also help. Rotted manure may well be applied to lettuce ground, but the use of fresh strawy manure should be avoided.

Spring lettuce should be started indoors or in a hotbed and transplanted to the garden when the plants have four or five leaves. Gardeners need not wait for the cessation of light frosts, as lettuce is not usually harmed by a temperature as low as 25° F. if the plants have been properly hardened. About six weeks should be allowed for growing the plants. Gardeners in northern Virginia, who set their plants in the open about April 15, must sow the seeds indoors about March 1. When plants can not be grown indoors or purchased, seeding should be done as early as the ground can be worked. For the fall crop the seed may be sown directly in the row and thinned, as there is no gain in transplanting.

For horse cultivation lettuce plants should be set 12 to 15 inches apart in rows 24 to 30 inches apart, and for hand culture about 12 to 15 inches apart each way. When the seed is sown directly in the row the plants should be thinned to the distances just mentioned. Where gardeners grow leaf lettuce, or desire merely the leaves and not well-developed heads, the spacing in the rows may be much closer. In any case it is usually best to cut the entire plant instead of removing the leaves.

There are many excellent varieties of lettuce, all of which do well in the garden when conditions are right. Of the loose-leaf kinds, Early Curled Simpson and Prize Head are among the best. Grown by the transplanting method described, individual plants of either of these may attain a weight of as much as $2\frac{1}{2}$ pounds. Of the heading sorts, May King, Unrivaled, Big Boston, New York, Iceberg, and Hanson are all excellent. Both New York and Iceberg need more time than May King, Unrivaled, and Big Boston. In regions where warm weather comes early, it is seldom worth while to sow head lettuce seed in the open ground in the spring with the expectation that firm heads will be obtained.

### PARSLEY

Parsley is hardy to cold but sensitive to heat. It will thrive under much the same temperature conditions as kale, lettuce, or spinach. If given a little protection it may be carried over winter throughout most of the North, but it can not withstand extreme heat.

Parsley will thrive on any good soil, but as the plant is delicate during its early stages of growth, the land should be mellow, not subject to baking, and free from clods and stones. In common with most vegetables, parsley needs plenty of soil fertility.

The seeds of parsley are small, and they germinate slowly. Soaking in water overnight will hasten germination. In northern locations it is a good plan to sow the seeds indoors and transplant the plants to the garden, thereby obtaining the crop ahead of hot weather. In the South it is usually possible to sow the seeds directly in drills. For the fall crop in the North, row seeding is also practiced. After seeding it is well to lay a board over the row for a few days until the first seedlings begin to appear. After its removal the plants should be watered from day to day to insure germination of as many seeds as possible. Parsley rows should be 14 to 16 inches apart, with the plants 4 to 5 inches apart in the rows.

The leaves of parsley are used for garnishing and for flavoring soups and vegetables. A few feet of row will supply the family, and a few plants transplanted to the coldframe in the autumn will give a supply during early spring.

### UPLAND CRESS

Upland cress, sometimes erroneously called peppergrass, is a hardy plant. It may be sown in all the milder portions of the country during autumn. In the colder sections it is sown during early spring as soon as the ground can be worked. The seeds are small and must not be covered deeply. After the plants are well established, thin to 4 to 6 inches apart in the rows. It is a short-season crop that should be planted in quick succession to insure a steady supply. The leaves and young shoots are used as a green salad or cooked like greens.

### WATER CRESS

Water cress is one of the few vegetable crops that can be grown in wet surroundings. In the more moderate portions of the North it grows practically the year round and winter is its best season in the South. It is best and most easily produced in water from springs in limestone regions; the limestone regions of Virginia, Maryland, Kentucky, and the Ozarks give almost ideal conditions. A supply for the family may be grown in a small spring-fed brook or a series of shallow pools where the water is about 1 foot deep. Care must be taken, though, to have a clean supply of water, otherwise the cress is unfit for use.

Water cress is started from seed and from pieces of plant. It is best to prepare the bed, using plenty of rotted manure, and turn the water on after the seeds or cuttings are in place. Early spring is the best time to plant water cress. Often seeds or cuttings may be placed in the rich, moist soil found at the edges of springs or brooks. No special care is required. The plant grows profusely in the wild state. A bed will yield a good crop the first season. Cress is used in salads for its pleasant pungency.

## ROOT AND TUBER-ROOT CROPS

Potatoes in the North and sweetpotatoes in the South are found in almost every garden. Other members of this group, especially beets, carrots, and turnips, are of almost the same importance. The vegetables in this classification may be used throughout the growing season and also be kept for winter. Without the supply of root crops from the home garden many families would have a restricted diet. They represent a very large proportion of the total value of home-garden crops.

### BEET

The beet is well adapted to all parts of the country. It is not especially sensitive to heat, and it is also resistant to cold; however, it will not withstand severe freezing, and in the lower South, where beets are usually grown the year round, they are sometimes killed by winter freezes. Farther north the winters are too severe, but spring, summer, and autumn culture is practiced. Owing to its wide adaptability and fine qualities, including the presence of vitamins B and C, the beet ranks near the top among home-garden vegetables.

The approximate time for sowing beets in the different parts of the country is shown in Table 1. As a rule, beets may be sown in the North as early as the ground can be worked in the spring; in the South they may be planted at almost any time, but midsummer heat and drought may interfere with germination. By covering the seeds with sandy soil, leaf mold, or some other material that will not bake, and by keeping the soil damp until the plants are up, much of this trouble can be avoided. Successive sowings should be made at intervals of about three weeks in order to have a continuous supply of young, tender beets throughout the season. Beets are sensitive to the reaction of the soil, and it is usually wise to apply lime if the soil is known to be strongly acid. Good quality depends upon quick development, and the land must be fertile, well drained, and in good physical condition. Well-rotted manure, supplemented by commercial fertilizer having a high proportion of both phosphorus and potash is recommended, both the manure and fertilizer to be applied broadcast before the seed is planted.

In gardens where cultivation is done by hand the rows may be about 16 inches apart; for horse cultivation they must be wider. Beet seed as purchased consists of small fruits each containing several seeds. These must be spaced thinly to avoid crowding. On most soils the seed should be covered to a depth of about an inch. After the plants are well established they should be thinned to stand 2 to 3 inches apart in the rows.

Early Wonder and Crosby Egyptian are standard varieties of beets suitable for early home-garden culture. Detroit Dark Red is an excellent variety for fall culture for winter use.[10]

### CARROT

Since about 1920 the carrot has made a remarkable rise in the esteem of gardeners. It was formerly grown mainly for storage for winter use, but the American housewife has learned to appreciate the worth of young, tender carrots, and they are now planted in succession and grown in much the same way as beets, thereby insuring a continuous supply of tender, succulent roots. From a dietetic standpoint carrots are particularly desirable, especially for children, as they are rich sources of vitamins A, B, and C. Moreover, they contain a yellow coloring matter known as carotin, which is also beneficial.

The carrot is hardy and is fairly resistant to heat. In the South carrots are largely grown during fall, winter, and spring, and gardeners in that part of the country can have a practically continuous supply. In the North the carrot can be grown and used throughout the summer and the surplus stored for winter. The carrot will grow on almost any type of soil as long as it is moist, fertile, loose, and free from clods and stones, but sandy loams and peats are best.

On account of their hardiness carrots may be seeded as early in the spring as the ground can be worked. Succession plantings at intervals of three weeks will insure a continuous supply of tender carrots. The application of coarse manure immediately before the carrot crop is planted is not advisable, as it makes the roots prongy and rough. Commercial fertilizer should be used. Planting distances are given in Table 3. Carrot seed should be covered about one-half inch on most soils; on heavy lands the depth should be less, usually about one-fourth inch. With care in seeding, little thinning is necessary, as carrots will stand some crowding, especially on loose soils. They should be no thicker than 15 to 20 plants per foot of row.

Chantenay, Nantes, and Danvers Half Long are standard sorts. Carrots should be stored before hard frosts occur, as the roots are injured by cold.

---

[10] Information on the storage of this and other root crops may be obtained from Farmers' Bulletin 879, Home Storage of Vegetables.

### CELERIAC

Celeriac, sometimes called turnip-rooted celery, has been developed for the root instead of the top. Its culture is the same as that of celery, and the enlarged roots can be used at any time after they attain sufficient size. Celeriac may be stored for winter use, but only the late summer crop should be used for storage. In regions having mild winters the roots may be left in the ground and covered with a mulch of several inches of straw or leaves, or they may be lifted and packed in moist sand and stored in a cool cellar.

### CHERVIL

Two distinct types of chervil are cultivated, the so-called salad chervil and the turnip-rooted chervil. The first is used for garnishing and for other purposes instead of parsley; by many it is considered superior to parsley. Its culture is practically the same as for parsley. The seeds must be bedded in damp sand for a few weeks before sowing, otherwise their germination is very slow.

Turnip-rooted chervil thrives in practically all parts of the country where fertile soil and sufficient moisture are to be had. In the South the seeds are usually sown during the fall but may not germinate until spring. In the North the seeds are sown during the autumn to germinate in the spring, or the plants are started indoors during late winter and transplanted to the open ground later on. Burying the seeds for a few weeks in damp sand materially hastens germination. Spacing and culture are about the same as for beets and carrots. Tables 1 and 2 give the approximate planting dates and the usual spacing of the crop.

### DASHEEN

The dasheen is closely related to the ordinary elephant ear. It is a long-season crop adapted for culture only in the lower South, where there is normally a very warm frostless season of at least seven months. It needs a rich loamy soil, an abundance of moisture with good drainage, and a fairly moist atmosphere. In portions of the South where it is adapted the dasheen is coming into prominence as a home and truck garden crop. Small tubers, those from 2 to 5 ounces in weight, are used for planting in much the same way as potatoes. Planting may be done two or three weeks before frosts are over, and the season may be lengthened by starting the plants indoors and setting them out after frost is past. The dasheen is a large-growing plant, similar in appearance to the well-known elephant ear, and the plants should be set in 3½ to 4 foot rows about 2 feet apart in the row. Dasheens may be dug and dried on the ground in much the same way as sweetpotatoes, and stored at 50° F. with ventilation. They are cooked and used in much the same way as potatoes.

### JERUSALEM ARTICHOKE

The Jerusalem artichoke is of interest to gardeners as a substitute for potatoes, but its tendency to become a weed should cause some caution in starting it. It is a near relative to the sunflower and can be grown practically throughout the United States. It is started from pieces of the tubers in the same way as potatoes. A quart of the tubers will set about 30 hills. The tubers are not injured by freezing and may remain in the ground over winter. Approximate planting dates are given in Table 1.

### PARSNIP

The parsnip is adapted to culture over a wide portion of the United States. While it must have warm soil and weather at planting time, it does not thrive in midsummer in the South, as the temperatures seem to be too high for it. Approximate dates for planting are given in Table 1. While both soil and weather conditions must be taken into account in selecting a planting date, some consideration must also be given to the length of the growing season. In many parts of the South parsnips are grown and used during early summer, but it would not pay to plant them at a season when they would come to maturity during midsummer. Moreover, it is difficult to obtain good germination during the summer, which limits their culture during the autumn. In the North it does not pay to plant parsnips too early or to give them too long a growing season, as they are liable to become oversize, tough, and fibrous.

Any deep fertile soil will grow parsnips, but those of a light, friable nature with no tendency to bake are best. Old garden land, spaded or plowed to a depth of about a foot and well enriched with fine well-rotted manure and commercial fertilizer, is almost ideal. Stony or lumpy soils are objectionable, as they are inclined to cause rough, prongy roots. Nor is coarse manure in direct contact with the roots advisable, for the same reason.

Spacing and seeding rates are given in Table 3. Parsnip seed must be fresh, that is, not over a year old, and it is well to sow rather thickly and thin to about 3 inches apart. Parsnips germinate slowly, but it is possible to help germination by covering the seed with leaf mold, sand, a mixture of sifted coal ashes and soil, peat, or some similar material that will not bake. Rolling the soil over the row or trampling it firmly after seeding usually hastens and improves germination. Boards are sometimes laid over the rows until the plants begin to come up. Hollow Crown and Guernsey are suitable varieties. The cultivation of parsnips is the same as that for similar crops.

Parsnips may be dug and stored in a cellar or pit or left in the ground until used. Roots placed in cold storage gain in quality faster than those left in the ground, and freezing in the ground in winter improves the quality. There is no basis for the belief that parsnips that remain in the ground over winter and start growth in the spring are poisonous. The reported cases of poisoning from eating so-called wild parsnips have all been traced to water hemlock (Cicuta), which belongs to the same family. The plant resembles the parsnip somewhat, and anyone should be very careful in gathering wild plants of this description.

### POTATO

Any good, well-drained garden soil is suitable for potato production. The crop needs much fertilizer and well-rotted manure. High-grade complete fertilizer may be advantageously applied to most soils for potatoes. Rates of application may be about the same as for other heavy-feeding vegetables, such as onions and cabbage. Preparation of soil for potatoes should be the same as for general garden crops.

In preparing seed potatoes it is desirable to cut them into blocky rather than wedge-shaped pieces. If good seed is scarce and high priced, it may be permissible to cut to single-eye pieces, provided the seed bed is especially well prepared and the conditions for germination are satisfactory. It should be remembered that the smaller the size of the seed piece the more necessary it becomes to have the growing conditions as favorable as possible.

Early potatoes should be planted as soon in the spring as the land can be worked, irrespective of locality. Late potatoes, extensively grown in the North, should be planted late in May or during June. The rows should be not less than 2 feet nor more than 3 feet apart and the hills 10 to 15 inches apart in the row. Lay off the rows with a 1-horse plow or lister, and drop the seed in the bottom of the furrow. Cover the seed to a depth of about 4 inches, using a hoe or a 1-horse plow. One to three weeks will be required for the potatoes to come up, depending entirely upon the temperature of the soil. The ground may freeze slightly after the planting has been done, but so long as the frost does not reach the seed potatoes no harm will result, and growth will begin as soon as the soil becomes sufficiently warm. Yields of potatoes may be materially increased by the use of certified seed that is relatively free from virus and other diseases. Certified seed is now sold by seedsmen and dealers almost everywhere, and its cost is only slightly above that of seed that has been grown without inspection or certification.

As soon as the potatoes appear above ground and the rows can be followed, the surface soil should be well stirred by means of one of the harrow-toothed cultivators. Good cultivation should be maintained throughout the growing season, with occasional hand hoeing, if necessary, to keep the ground free from weeds. After the vines begin to die, the soil may be well worked up around the plants in order to hold them erect and protect the tubers from the sun.

After the potatoes are dug they should not be allowed to lie exposed to the sun or to any light while in storage, as they soon become green and unfit for table use. Early potatoes especially should not be stored in a damp place during the heat of summer and will keep best if covered with straw in a cool, shady shed until autumn weather sets in, after which they can be placed in a dry cellar or buried in the open ground. The ideal temperature for keeping potatoes is between 40° and 45° F., but they will not withstand any freezing.[11]

### RADISH

Radishes are hardy but they can not withstand heat. In the South they do well during the autumn, winter, and spring, but do not thrive in summer. In the North they may be grown in the spring and autumn, and in sections having mild winters they may

---

[11] For additional information on potatoes, consult the following Farmers' Bulletins: No. 1205, Potato Production in the South; No. 1064, Production of Late or Main-Crop Potatoes; No. 1190, How to Grow an Acre of Potatoes; No. 1371, Diseases and Insects of Garden Vegetables; No. 879, Home Storage of Vegetables; No. 847, Potato Storage and Storage Houses.

be grown in coldframes at this season. In high altitudes and in northern locations having cool summers, they will thrive from early spring to late autumn.

Radishes are not sensitive to the type of soil, so long as it is rich, moist, and friable. Fertility from decayed manure and commercial fertilizer is essential. Some additional fertility applied when the seeds are sown is advisable, as conditions must be favorable for quick growth. Radishes that grow slowly have a pungent flavor and are undesirable.

Radishes mature the quickest of our garden crops. They remain in prime condition only a few days, and the gardener should plan to make small plantings every two weeks. A few yards of row will supply all the radishes a family will consume during the time they are at their best. Tables 1, 2, and 3 give approximate planting dates, rates of seeding, and spacing. Care in spacing the seeds saves labor in thinning.

There are two types of radishes, the mild, small, quick-maturing sorts, such as Scarlet Globe, French Breakfast, and Cincinnati Market, all of which reach edible size in from 20 to 40 days; and the more pungent, large, so-called winter radishes, such as Long Black Spanish and Rose China, which require 75 days or more for growth. These latter are planted so as to reach a desirable size in the autumn and are gathered and stored like other root crops. Winter radishes deserve the attention of more gardeners.

### SALSIFY

Salsify, or vegetable oyster, has a wide adaptation and may be grown in practically all parts of the country. It is very similar to parsnips in its requirements but needs a slightly longer growing season. For this reason it can not be grown as far north as parsnips. Salsify, however, is somewhat more hardy and can be sown earlier in the spring.

Soil for salsify should be thoroughly pulverized to a depth of at least a foot. If heavy, the garden soil should be lightened by adding sifted coal ashes, sand, or some other material. Like parsnips, salsify must have plenty of plant food, but fresh, rough manure should be avoided, as this causes rough, prongy roots.

Sandwich Island is the best-known variety. An ounce of seed will sow a 100-foot row, and a 50-foot row will meet the requirements of most families. As salsify seed retains its vitality only one year, fresh seed should always be used. Approximate dates for sowing are given in Table 1. Width of rows, depth of planting, and the stand in the rows are given in Table 3.

Cultivation is the same as for other root crops. Salsify may be left in the ground over winter or lifted and stored like parsnips or other root crops. This fine vegetable should be grown more generally.

### SWEETPOTATO

The sweetpotato is of tropical origin and succeeds best in the South. It is grown in home gardens as far north as southern New York and Michigan. Even farther north, in sections having especially mild climates, such as the Pacific Northwest, sweetpotato culture is possible. In general, sweetpotatoes may be grown in any locality where there is a frost-free period of about 150 days with relatively high temperature. The plant succeeds with a minimum supply of moisture, differing in this respect from many other home-garden vegetables.

A well-drained, moderately deep sandy soil of medium fertility is best for sweetpotatoes. Very deep, open soils encourage the formation of long stringy roots and should be avoided. To improve drainage the plants usually are set on top of wide ridges. For best results the soil should be moderately fertilized throughout, but most areas that have been used for home gardening probably will produce a good crop of sweetpotatoes without additional fertilization. A little well-rotted manure and some commercial fertilizer may be advantageously applied to poor soils. If applied under the rows, both manure and fertilizer should be well mixed with the soil.

Toward the northern part of the area over which sweetpotatoes are grown it is necessary to start the plants in a hotbed, because the season is too short to produce a crop after the weather warms enough to start plants out of doors. The roots too small for marketing are used for seed, bedded close together in the hotbed, and covered with about 2 inches of sand or fine soil such as leaf mold. The seed should be bedded about five or six weeks before it is safe to set the plants in the open ground. Toward the last the hotbed should be ventilated freely to harden off the plants.

The ridges for planting sweetpotatoes should be 3 to 5 feet apart and the plants about 14 inches apart in the row. Cultivate sufficiently to keep the surface soil loose and free from weeds. As soon as the vines cover the ground no cultivation is necessary.

Sweetpotatoes are dug as soon as the vines are nipped by frost. They should be dug on a bright, drying day, when the soil is not too wet. On a small scale they may be dug with a spading fork, great care being taken not to bruise or injure the roots. The roots should lie exposed for two or three hours to dry thoroughly, after which they may be placed in a warm, well-ventilated room to cure for several days. The proper temperature for curing is 80° to 90° F. for about 10 days, and then store them at 50° to 55° afterwards. A small crop may be cured around the kitchen stove and later stored in a dry room where there is no danger of their becoming too cold. Sweetpotatoes should be handled as little as possible, especially after they are cured.[12]

#### TURNIP AND RUTABAGA

Turnips and rutabagas are similar and are treated together. They are among the most commonly grown and widely adapted root crops in the United States. Being essentially cool-weather vegetables, they are grown in the South chiefly during the fall, winter, and spring, while in the North their culture is confined largely to the spring and autumn. Rutabaga does best in the more northerly locations, and gardeners south of the latitude of Indianapolis, Ind., or northern Virginia are advised to grow turnips instead.

---

[12] For additional information on sweetpotatoes, the following Farmers' Bulletins may be consulted: No. 999, Sweet-Potato Growing; No. 1059, Sweet-Potato Diseases; No. 1442, Storage of Sweet Potatoes; and No. 879, Home Storage of Vegetables.

Turnips reach a good size in from 60 to 80 days, but rutabagas need about a month longer. Being susceptible to heat and hardy, these crops for fall use should be planted as late as possible, allowing time for maturity before hard frost. In the South, turnips are very popular during the winter and spring, but in the North fall seeding following early potatoes, peas, or spinach is usually practiced.

Both turnips and rutabagas need a fertile soil. However, land that has been in some heavily fertilized crop, such as early potatoes, usually gives a good crop without additional fertilization. The soil need not be prepared deeply, but the surface should be fine and smooth. For spring culture, row planting similar to that described for beets should be practiced. The importance of planting turnips as early as possible for the spring crop is emphasized. When seeding in rows, cover the seeds lightly; and when broadcasting, rake the seeds in with a garden rake. A half ounce of seed will sow a 100-foot row or broadcast 100 square feet. Turnips may be thinned as they grow, and the tops used for greens.

The common varieties of turnip and rutabaga differ mainly in color and shape of root. Although there are both white-fleshed and yellow-fleshed varieties of each, most turnips are white-fleshed, while most rutabaga varieties are yellow-fleshed. Both may have white, green, or purplish red crowns. Purple-Top Strap Leaf and Purple-Top White Milan are well-known white-fleshed turnips. Golden Ball and Petrowski are good yellow-fleshed sorts. American Purple-Top is a yellow-fleshed rutabaga, and White Russian or Sweet Russian is a white-fleshed rutabaga.

### TURNIP-ROOTED PARSLEY

The root is the edible portion of turnip-rooted parsley. It has a superficial resemblance to the parsnip, and the flesh is whitish and dry, with much the same flavor as celeriac. It is boiled and used like celeriac or other root crops.

Turnip-rooted parsley requires the same climate, soil, and culture as parsley. It is hardy and able to withstand much cold, but is difficult to start in dry, hot weather. The seeds are small and usually germinate slowly. It is well to soak them in water overnight before sowing and to mix them with dry sand to obtain better distribution in the rows. The plants should be thinned to about 3 inches apart in the rows. Planting dates and spacing are given in Tables 1 and 3. This vegetable may remain in the ground until after hard frosts. It may be lifted and stored like other root crops.

### VINE CROPS (CUCURBITS)

The vine crops, including cucumbers, muskmelons, pumpkins, squashes, watermelons, and citrons, are grouped together because of the similarity of their culture. In importance to the home gardener they do not compare with some other groups, especially the root crops and the greens, but there is a place in most gardens for at least bush squashes and a few hills of cucumbers. In large gardens a few hills of muskmelons and watermelons are often desirable.

## CUCUMBER

The cucumber is distinctly a warm-weather crop. It may be grown during the warmer months over a wide portion of the country, but it is not adapted to winter growing in any but a few of the most southerly locations. Moreover, the extreme heat of midsummer in some locations is too severe, and cucumber culture in these regions is limited to spring and autumn. Tables 1 and 2 give the approximate dates when cucumbers may be planted in the various sections.

The cucumber demands an exceedingly fertile, mellow soil. In addition to the manuring and fertilization suggested in an earlier portion of this bulletin, some well-rotted manure and commercial fertilizer is advisable under the rows or hills, but the gardener should be sure that the manure contains no remains of any vine crops, as these might carry injurious diseases. Three or four wheelbarrow loads of manure and 5 pounds of commercial fertilizer to a 50-foot drill or each 10 hills is enough. The manure and fertilizer should be well mixed with the top 8 to 10 inches of soil.

Cucumbers are sensitive to cold, and they should not be planted until the ground has warmed up. For an early crop the seed may be started in berry boxes, plant bands, pots, or on sods in a hotbed, and moved to the garden after danger of late frost is past. During early growth and in cool periods cucumbers and other tender plants may be covered with plant protectors made of panes of glass with a top of cheesecloth, parchment paper, or muslin. A few hills will supply the family with pickling and slicing stock, and the few precautions necessary to insure success are well repaid.

Cucumbers make a rank growth and must have plenty of room. When planted in drills, the rows should be 6 or 7 feet apart, with the plants thinned to 2 to 3 feet apart in the rows. With the hill method of planting, the hills should be at least 6 feet apart each way, with the plants thinned to two to each hill. It is always wise to plant 8 or 10 seeds in each hill, thinning to the desired stand. Cucumber seeds should be covered to a depth of about 1 inch; and if the soil is inclined to bake they should be covered with loose earth, such as a mixture of soil and sifted coal ashes, sand, or other material that will not harden and keep the plants from coming through.

When grown primarily for pickling, one of the special small-sized pickling varieties, such as Chicago Pickling or Snow's Pickling, should be used; if for slicing, such varieties as White Spine and Early Fortune should be employed. It is usually desirable to plant a few hills of each type, but the slicing type can be planted and used for both purposes.

Cucumbers require almost constant vigilance to prevent destructive attacks by cucumber beetles. These insects not only eat the foliage but also spread cucumber wilt and other serious diseases. During the early stages of growth the plants may be protected by small frames such as a wooden barrel hoop tacked to three pegs and covered with cheesecloth or mosquito netting, the edges of the netting being covered with earth to keep it from blowing off and to prevent insects from gaining entrance. The covering may be removed while cultivating, but it must be immediately replaced, as no insects should be allowed to touch the plants. When the vines begin to run, the covering must be removed. Thorough dusting with an arsenical dust every few days helps to control cucumber beetles. For the melon aphis, another serious enemy, a nicotine dust should be used, or a combined application may be made for both.[13]

The removal of the fruits before any hard seeds form materially lengthens the life of the plants and the size of the crop.

### MUSKMELON

The muskmelon needs an abundance of room, and its culture in gardens where space is scarce is seldom justified. In the larger home gardens or in the home truck patch where conditions are suitable, the muskmelon is a desirable addition to the list of crops. The climatic and soil requirements of the muskmelon are about the same as for the cucumber. It seems to develop more perfectly when grown on light-textured soils, whereas the cucumber does well on moderately heavy land. The plants are vigorous growers, and the spacing should be somewhat wider than for cucumbers. Table 3 gives the width of rows and spacing.

Muskmelons are frequently started indoors in pots, berry boxes, plant bands, or in pieces of sod and transferred to the garden later. In sections where the growing season is short or earliness desired, this practice is important. Special precautions should be taken to protect muskmelons from attacks by insects. This can be accomplished as suggested for cucumbers.

Hearts of Gold, Emerald Gem, Pollock 10-25, and Tiptop are standard varieties of the common muskmelon. Several special types of melons such as the Casaba, Honeydew, and Persian are being grown to some extent in various parts of the United States. In general, these are not well adapted to home-garden culture except in certain portions of the South and West, where they are produced under irrigation.[14]

### PUMPKIN

Pumpkins are sensitive to both cold and heat. In the North they can not be planted until settled weather has arrived; in the South they do not thrive during midsummer. Approximate planting dates for different sections are given in Table 1.

Most varieties of pumpkins require an abundance of room. The gardener, therefore, is seldom justified in devoting any portion of a limited garden area to pumpkins, because many other vegetables would give greater returns from the same area. However, in large gardens where there is plenty of room and where they can be planted after some early crop like potatoes, it is often possible to grow pumpkins to advantage. If planted in hills, they should be at least 10 feet apart each way, but when started among corn, potato, or other plants they are usually spaced 8 to 10 feet apart in every third or fourth row.

The pumpkin is one of the few vegetables that thrives under partial shade and for this reason may be grown among sweet corn or other

---

[13] For additional information on cucumber culture and cucumber enemies, see Farmers' Bulletins 1563, Cucumber Growing, and 1371, Diseases and Insects of Garden Vegetables.
[14] For additional information on muskmelon culture, see Farmers' Bulletin 1468, Muskmelons.

tall-growing plants. Small Sugar and Connecticut Field are well-known orange-yellow skinned varieties. The Kentucky Cheese has a grayish orange color with salmon-colored flesh. All are good-quality, productive varieties.

Pumpkins should be gathered and stored before they are injured by hard frosts. They keep best in a well-ventilated place where the temperature is a little above 50° F.

### SQUASH

Squashes are among the most commonly grown garden plants. They may be grown in practically all parts of the United States where fertile soil with sufficient moisture is found. Soils rich in organic matter are needed. The use of well-rotted manure thoroughly mixed with the soil is recommended. Although sensitive to frost, they are more hardy than melons and cucumbers. In the warmer portions of the South squashes may be grown during the winter.

There are two classes of squash varieties, summer and winter. The former includes the Bush Scallop, known in some localities as the Cymling, and the Summer Crookneck. The winter class includes the hard-shelled, later-maturing storage varieties such as Hubbard, Delicious, and Boston Marrow. The so-called vegetable marrows are also classed as summer squashes. Italian Vegetable Marrow, or Cocozelle, is the best-known sort. All the summer squashes and the marrows must be used while young and tender, easily penetrated by the thumb nail. The winter squashes have hard rinds and are well adapted for storage.

The summer varieties, such as Crookneck and Bush Scallop, are of the bush type and may be planted early. If in drills, the rows should be about 5 feet apart with the plants spaced 18 inches in the rows. If in hills, these should be about 4 by 4 feet with two plants in each hill. Such varieties as Boston Marrow and Hubbard should be in drills 10 to 12 feet apart or in hills 8 by 8 to 12 by 12 feet apart.

Summer varieties should be gathered before the seeds ripen or the rinds harden, but the winter sorts will not keep unless well matured. They should be taken in before hard frosts occur and stored in a dry, moderately warm place, such as on shelves in a basement with a furnace. Under favorable conditions such varieties as Hubbard may be kept until midwinter.[15]

### WATERMELON

Like muskmelons and pumpkins, watermelons require an abundance of room, and only the larger gardeners can afford to devote space to them. Moreover, watermelons are rather sensitive to the soil on which they are grown, a sand or sandy loam being practically essential. Being warm-weather plants, it is useless to plant the seeds too early or to attempt their culture in sections where the season is too short and the temperature too low. The approximate time for planting watermelons in the different zones is given in Table 1. Watermelon hills should be at least 10 feet apart; consequently a few hills take up a large amount of space. The old plan of making the hills by mixing a half wheelbarrow load of rotted manure with

---

[15] For additional information on squashes and pumpkins, ask for the mimeographed circular on these subjects prepared by the Division of Horticultural Crops and Diseases, Bureau of Plant Industry, U. S. Department of Agriculture.

the soil in each hill is a good one, provided the manure is free from the remains of cucurbit plants that might carry disease. A half pound of commercial fertilizer also should be thoroughly mixed with the soil in the hill. It is a good plan to place several seeds in a ring about 1 foot in diameter in each hill. Later the plants should be thinned, two to each hill.

Kleckley Sweet, Florida Favorite, Stone Mountain, and Tom Watson are suitable varieties for the home garden.

The preserving type of watermelon, called citron, is not edible when raw. Its culture is the same as that for the watermelon.

## LEGUMES

Beans and peas are among our oldest and most important garden plants. They contain large quantities of fats and proteins, and only a limited space is required for growing the family supply. Both beans and peas, especially in the fresh green state, as one can have them from the home garden, are among the richest sources of vitamins A, B, and C. Recent investigations have revealed that they also contain other beneficial vitamins. The popularity of both beans and peas is also due in part to their wide climatic and soil adaptation.

### BEANS

From the home gardener's point of view green beans, both snap and Lima, are of more importance than dry beans. Green snap beans are among the most important vegetables grown in the garden. In the North snap beans can not be planted until the ground is thoroughly warm, but succession plantings may be made every two weeks from that time until a few weeks before frost. In the South and Southwest green beans may be grown over a wide portion of the fall, winter, and spring seasons, but they are not well adapted to midsummer. In the extreme South beans are grown throughout the winter. The approximate dates for planting beans in the different zones are given in Table 1, and the spacing and quantity of seed needed are shown in Table 3.

Green beans are not especially sensitive to the character of the soil upon which they are grown, as long as it is well drained, reasonably fertile, and of such physical nature that it does not interfere with germination and emergence of the plants. Soil that has received a general application of manure and fertilizer should need no additional fertilization. When beans follow early crops that have been fertilized the residue of this fertilizer is usually sufficient for the beans.

As it develops the bean plant pushes the two halves of the seed, or cotyledons, through the surface, and heavy-textured soils that bake are liable to interfere seriously with or prevent normal development. On heavy lands it is well to cover the seeds with sand, a mixture of sifted coal ashes and sand, peat, leaf mold, or some other material that will not bake. By keeping the surface of the ground moist but not too wet for a few days after planting the plants may be brought up without difficulty. It is very important that bean seed be covered not more than 1 inch in heavy soils and 1½ inches on sandy soils. Beans are sensitive to cold and should never be planted until the soil has warmed up and the weather is settled. The dates given for planting beans and other tender crops must often be changed to suit the season. When beans are planted in hills they may be covered with plant protectors, thereby making it possible to plant somewhat earlier than otherwise.

Burpee Stringless Green Pod and Hodson Kidney Wax are good bush varieties for use as snap or green beans. Kentucky Wonder is a good pole sort for the same use. Any of these may be dried and kept for winter. If intended primarily for use dry, White Navy and Dwarf Horticultural are excellent sorts.

Two types of Lima or so-called butter beans are grown in home gardens. In the North the large Lima (*Phaseolus lunatus macrocarpus*) is most generally grown. In the South the Sieva or Carolina type is mainly grown. Certain more northerly sections of the United States, including northern New England and the northern portions of the States along the Canadian border, are not adapted to the culture of Lima beans. Lima beans should have a growing season of about four months with relatively high temperature and can not be planted with safety until somewhat later than snap beans. Weather and soil conditions must be suitable before it is safe to put the seeds in the ground. The small butter beans will mature in a shorter period than the large-seeded Lima beans. By starting the seed indoors in berry baskets or other containers and moving them to the open ground when the weather is settled, a little may be gained in earliness. The use of plant protectors over the seeds will also aid in obtaining earliness. In the South planting dates depend upon location. In the lower South, however, midsummer plantings are seldom practicable, and in the northerly portions planting is restricted to spring and early summer.

Lima beans may be grown on almost any fertile, well-drained, mellow soil, but it is especially desirable that the soil be light-textured and not subject to baking, as the plants can not force their way through a hard crust. Covering with some material that will not bake, as suggested for other beans, is a wise precaution when using heavy soils. Lima beans need a soil somewhat richer than is necessary for kidney beans, but the excessive use of manure or fertilizer containing a high percentage of nitrogen should be avoided. Beans do well when supplied with a fertilizer containing a relatively high proportion of phosphoric acid.

Both the Sieva and the large Lima are to be had in pole and bush forms. Bush beans may be drilled in rows like green beans; pole Lima beans require more room than the bush forms. Precautions must be taken to avoid covering Lima bean seed too deep. From 1 inch to 1½ inches is about the right depth.

In the South Henderson Bush Lima and the Small White Lima (a pole bean) are commonly used; in the North Henderson Bush Lima, Burpee Bush Lima, Siebert Pole Lima, King of the Garden, and Emerald Isle (pole beans) are largely used.

Pole beans of the kidney and Lima types require some form of support, as they normally make vines several feet long. The well-known bean pole consisting of a small sapling about 2 inches in diameter at the base and 6 or 7 feet long is very satisfactory. Sawed stakes are objectionable on account of the corners and their smoothness, which makes it difficult for the beans to climb. Beans usually need some help in getting started up the poles. They twine in a counterclockwise direction. Where poles are difficult to obtain beans may be trained to a trellis made of a top and bottom wire stretched between posts and connected every foot or two by stout twine. Some gardeners plant pole beans along the fence or beside hills of corn, which serve as supports.

The only special precaution to observe in cultivating beans is to avoid cultivating or handling the vines while wet, as this is liable to spread disease. The advent of the Mexican bean beetle in the East has brought the home gardener in these sections face to face with a difficult problem. Spraying or dusting with magnesium arsenate is recommended.[16]

### PEAS

Peas have many of the merits possessed by beans. They are high in food value and rich sources of vitamins A, B, and C. They require more space than beans, and with limited garden areas only an early planting may be practicable. Fresh-picked peas are so superior in quality to those that have been off the plants for some time that every gardener who has the space and can grow them should include peas in his list of vegetables.

Peas are distinctly a cool-weather crop. In the lower South they are grown at all seasons except during the summer; farther north the seasons for peas are spring and autumn. In the northern tier of States and at high altitudes they may be grown from spring until autumn, although in many places summer heat is too severe and the season is practically limited to spring. Table 1 gives the approximate date for planting peas in the different zones. A good general rule to follow in portions of the South where freezing does not occur is to plant at any time except in the warmer months. In the North the best general rule is to plant as early as the ground can be worked, and a few succession plantings may be made at 10-day intervals. The later plantings rarely yield as well as the earlier ones. Plantings may be resumed as the cool weather of autumn approaches, but the yield is seldom as satisfactory as that from the spring crop. Planting distances and depth of covering for peas are given in Table 3.

Alaska and Long Pod Alaska are small-growing early sorts of smooth peas. Gradus, Thomas Laxton, and Telephone are wrinkled kinds that should be used for later harvests. Telephone and other varieties having a heavy vine growth require more space and some form of support, such as brush stuck in the ground, wire fencing stretched between end posts and supported every few feet by stakes, a trellis, or some other inexpensive device. To enjoy the utmost quality in garden peas, gather them while sweet and tender, and cook and serve within the hour.

### CABBAGE GROUP

The cabbage or cole group includes heading broccoli, sprouting broccoli, Brussels sprouts, cabbage, Chinese cabbage, cauliflower,

---

[16] For information on insects and diseases of beans see Farmers' Bulletin 1371, Diseases and Insects of Garden Vegetables. For information on the Mexican bean beetle and its control, see Farmers' Bulletin 1407, The Mexican Bean Beetle in the East and Its Control.

collards, and kohlrabi. These plants are noteworthy because of their adaptation to culture in most portions of the country where fertile soil and sufficient moisture are to be found and because of their hardiness to cold and richness in vitamins A, B, and C. Altogether they are among the most valuable of the home-garden crops.

#### HEADING BROCCOLI

Heading broccoli is similar to cauliflower in appearance—even being marketed as cauliflower—but it needs a much longer period for development. In the South and certain portions of the West, broccoli plants may be set in summer and autumn and come to edible maturity during late winter and early spring. In the colder portions of the North it will not live over winter, and the growing season is not long enough for most varieties of broccoli. Early Large White French is one of the best-known varieties. In soil and cultural requirements broccoli is similar to cauliflower.

#### SPROUTING BROCCOLI

Sprouting broccoli is a kind that forms a loose flower head upon a tall, fleshy, branching stalk instead of compact heads or curds as in the case with both cauliflower and heading broccoli. This is one of the newer vegetables to most American gardeners, but it has been known and appreciated by Europeans for many years.

Sprouting broccoli is adapted to winter culture in regions suitable for wintering-over cabbage. It is also very resistant to heat. Spring-set plants in the latitude of Washington, D. C., have yielded good crops of sprouts until midsummer and later, under conditions that caused cauliflower to fail. In the latitude of Norfolk, Va., the plant has yielded good crops of sprouts from December until spring. It is an exceptionally promising home-garden crop.

Sprouting broccoli is grown in the same way as cabbage. Plants grown indoors during the early spring and set in the open about April 1 begin to yield sprouts about 10 weeks later. The fall crop may be handled in the same way as late cabbage, except that the seed is sown later. The sprouts carrying flower buds are cut about 6 inches long, and other sprouts arise in the axils of the leaves so that a continuous harvest may be obtained. The habits of growth are shown in Figure 19. Italian Green Sprouting is one of the best-known varieties or strains.

#### BRUSSELS SPROUTS

Brussels sprouts are somewhat more hardy than cabbage and will live outdoors over winter in all the milder sections of the country. It may be grown as a winter crop in the South and as early and late cabbage in the North. The sprouts, or small heads, are formed in the axils of the leaves. (Fig. 20.) As the heads begin to crowd, the lower leaves should be broken from the stem of the plant to give them more room. The top leaves should always be left, as the plant needs them to supply nourishment. For winter use in cold climates, take up the plants that are well laden with heads and set them close together in a pit, a coldframe, or a cellar with some soil tamped around the roots. Keep the stored plants as cool as possible without freezing.

FIGURE 19.—Sprouting broccoli, a worth-while addition to the list of garden vegetables

## CABBAGE

Because of its wide climatic and soil adaptability and its popularity as a food, cabbage undoubtedly ranks as one of the most important home-garden crops. In the lower South it can be grown in all seasons except during the summer, and in latitudes as far north as Washington, D. C., it is frequently set during the autumn, as its extreme hardiness enables it to live over winter at relatively low temperatures and thus become available among the first garden crops of spring. Farther north it can be grown as an early summer crop and as a late fall crop for storage. Unlike many other garden crops, cabbage can be grown throughout practically the entire United States where suitable soil and sufficient moisture are to be found.

Cabbage is not at all sensitive to the type of soil on which it is grown so long as the land is very fertile, of good texture, and moist. Cabbage is a gross feeder, and no vegetable will make a greater or more rapid response to favorable growing conditions. Quality in cabbage is closely associated with quick growth, and both rotted manure or compost and commercial fertilizer should be liberally used. In addition to the applications made at planting time, cabbage may also received a side dressing or two of nitrate of soda, sulphate of ammonia, or some other quickly available nitrogenous

FIGURE 20.—Brussels sprouts. The sprouts are borne in the axils of the leaves

fertilizer. These may be applied sparingly to the soil around the plants at intervals of three weeks, not more than 1 pound being used to each 200 square feet of space, or, in terms of single plants, a third of an ounce to each plant. For late cabbage the soil should not be so rich, and the supplemental feeding with nitrates may be omitted.

Good seed is especially important. Only a few cents' worth of seed is needed for starting enough plants for the home garden, as two or three dozen heads of early cabbage are as many as the average family can use. Early Jersey Wakefield and Charleston Wakefield are standard early sorts. Copenhagen Market and All Seasons are excellent midseason kinds, while for late cabbage Flat Dutch and Danish Ball Head are largely used.

Where cabbage yellows is a serious trouble, resistant varieties should be used. The following are a few of the wilt-resistant varieties adapted to different seasons: Wisconsin Hollander, for late storage; Wisconsin All Seasons, somewhat earlier, a kraut cabbage; Marion Market, for midseason, a round-head cabbage; Globe, for midseason, a round-head cabbage.

Cabbage plants for spring setting in the North may be grown in hotbeds or greenhouses from seeding made a month to six weeks before planting time, or may be purchased from southern growers who produce them outdoors during winter. These winter-grown, hardened plants, sometimes referred to as "frost proof," are hardier than hotbed plants and may be set outdoors in most portions of the North as soon as the ground can be worked in the spring. Northern gardeners can have cabbage from their gardens much earlier by using healthy southern-grown plants or well-hardened, well-grown hotbed, or greenhouse plants. Late cabbage, prized by northern gardeners for fall use and for storage, is grown from plants produced in open seed beds from sowings made about a month ahead of planting. Late cabbage may well follow early potatoes, peas, beets, spinach, or some other early crop. Many gardeners set cabbage plants between potato rows before the potatoes are ready to dig, thereby gaining time. The approximate date for setting cabbage plants is given in Table 1. In protected locations or if plant protectors are used, it is possible always to advance dates somewhat, especially if the plants are well hardened. Planting distances for cabbage are given in Table 3.[17]

Late cabbage is one of the most satisfactory vegetables for storage for winter. The heads may be cut and packed in a barrel or a box buried in the ground or covered with soil, or the plants may be pulled and buried in a low windrow.

### CHINESE CABBAGE

Chinese cabbage, which is closely related to both cabbage and turnips, is variously known as pai tsai, petsay, pe-tsai, pok choi, wong bok, etc. The name celery cabbage is popularly applied to it, although it is unrelated to celery. Another form, which might be called the nonheading type of Chinese cabbage, has been erroneously

---

[17] Complete information on the culture, storage, and enemies of cabbage is to be found in the following Farmers' Bulletins: No. 433, Cabbage; No. 879, Home Storage of Vegetables; No. 1371, Diseases and Insects of Garden Vegetables.

called white Chinese mustard. It does not form a head, but is grown for a potherb. The nonheading types are popular and deserve greater attention.

Chinese cabbage seems to do best as an autumn crop in the northern tier of States. When well grown, it is an attractive vegetable. It is not especially successful as a spring crop, and gardeners are advised to confine their attention to its fall culture in the North and its winter culture in the South.

The plant demands a very rich, well-drained, but moist soil. The seeds may be sown and the plants transplanted to the garden, or they may be drilled in the garden rows and the plants thinned to the desired stand. For the fall crop in the North, about two and one-half months before frost is a good time to sow the seeds. The approximate dates for sowing are given in Tables 1 and 2, and the spacing of the plants and depth of covering seeds are given in Table 3.

## CAULIFLOWER

FIGURE 21.—A good head of cauliflower

Cauliflower has been called "rich man's cabbage," because it is more difficult to grow. It has an attractive appearance during growth and as prepared for the table. (Fig. 21.) Although hardy, it will not withstand as much frost as cabbage. Any considerable degree of warm weather is fatal to cauliflower, causing it to fail to head. In the South its culture is limited to fall, winter, and spring; in the North it is practically confined to spring and autumn, as the summers and winters are too severe. However, in some regions of high altitude and when conditions are otherwise favorable cauliflower culture is continuous throughout the summer. In most cases it is treated as an early and a late crop in much the same way as cabbage.

Like cabbage, cauliflower requires a fertile, well-drained soil. It is grown on all types of land from sands to clays and peats. Although the physical character is unimportant, the land must be fertile. Manure and commercial fertilizer are thus essential.

The time required for growing cauliflower plants is the same as for cabbage. In the North the main cause of failure with cauliflower in the spring is in not sowing the seed and setting the plants early enough. The fall crop must be planted at such a time that it will come to the heading stage during cool weather. Tables 1 and 2 give the approximate planting dates for cauliflower in the various zones. Snowball and Dwarf Erfurt are standard varieties of cauliflower.

Care should always be taken to obtain a good strain of seed; poor cauliflower seed is especially objectionable.

The only special precaution to be observed in the culture of cauliflower is to tie the leaves together when the heads or "buttons" begin to form, in order to keep the heads white. Cauliflower does not keep long after the heads form, and a dozen or two heads are sufficient for the average gardener.[18]

### COLLARDS

The culture and uses of collards are the same as for cabbage. Collards withstand the heat better than other members of the cabbage group, and they are highly esteemed in the South for both summer and winter use. Collards do not form a true head, but instead a large rosette of leaves, which may be blanched by tying together or covering.

### KOHLRABI

The edible portion of kohlrabi consists of the swollen stem of the plant. The early crop in the North may be started like cabbage and transplanted to the garden. In the South kohlrabi may be grown at almost any time during the year except midsummer. The approximate dates for planting and the spacing of the plants in the rows are given in Tables 1, 2, and 3. Kohlrabi seeds may be started indoors and the plants transplanted to the garden, or the seeds may be drilled in the garden rows and the plants thinned to the desired stand. In soil and cultural requirements kohlrabi is similar to cabbage. The principal requirements are fertile soil and sufficient moisture. Kohlrabi is an excellent vegetable if harvested while young and tender.

### ONION GROUP

Onions and related plants are among the oldest and most popular of the home-garden crops. It would be difficult to find a home garden without at least one of this group, which includes chive, garlic, leek, onion, and shallot. Practically all of these have an exceedingly wide soil and climatic adaptation; at least some can be grown in all parts of the country where fertile soil and sufficient moisture are found.

The members of the onion group require but little garden space to produce enough for the family needs. They may be grown over a large part of the season, and dry onions are well adapted to winter storage. Moreover, these plants are good sources of vitamins A, B, and C.

### CHIVES

The chive is a small onionlike plant that is used for flavoring soups and stews. (Fig. 22.) The plants will grow in any place where onions do well. They are frequently planted as a border, but they are equally adapted to culture in rows like other vegetables. Being a perennial, chive should be planted in a place where it can be left for more than one season. The approximate planting date in different zones is given in Tables 1 and 2, and spacing information is given in Table 3.

---

[18] For additional information on the culture of cauliflower, send for a mimeographed circular prepared by the Division of Horticultural Crops and Diseases, Bureau of Plant Industry, U. S. Department of Agriculture.

Chive may be started from either seed or clumps of bulbs. When once established, it is an easy matter to lift some of the bulbs and move them to a new location. When left in the same place for several years they become too thick, and an occasional resetting is desirable.

### GARLIC

Garlic is more exacting in its cultural requirements than are onions, but it may be grown with a fair degree of success in almost any home garden where good results are obtained with other vegetables. Like chive, garlic is of value chiefly for seasoning; and while desirable as an addition to the list of garden crops, it must be considered of minor importance.

The approximate planting dates and spacing are given in Tables 1, 2, and 3. Garlic is propagated by planting the small cloves or bulbs which make up the large bulbs. Each large bulb contains about 10 small ones. In preparing the stock for planting, the small bulbs are carefully separated and planted singly. Each will grow into a bulb containing about 10 small ones. (Fig. 23.)

FIGURE 22.—A clump of chive

The culture of garlic is practically the same as that for onions. When mature the bulbs are pulled, dried, and braided into strings or tied in bunches, which are hung in a cool, well-ventilated place for later use. In the South, where the crop matures early, care must be taken to keep the garlic under favorable conditions, otherwise it will spoil. In the North, where the crop matures later in the season, storage is not so difficult, but care must be taken to prevent freezing.

FIGURE 23.—Garlic. Each bulb contains several small ones. These are separated for planting

### LEEK

The leek is very similar to the onion in its adaptability and cultural requirements. It forms a thick fleshy structure like a large green onion instead of a bulb. (Fig. 24.) This is used in soups and stews and for almost any purpose to which the onion is adapted. Leeks are started from seeds like onions, but are usually sown in a trench, so that the plants can be more easily hilled up as growth proceeds. Tables 1, 2, and 3 give planting dates and spacing distances. Leeks are ready for use any time after they attain suitable size, but under favorable conditions they grow to 1½ inches or more in diameter, with white stalks 6 to 8 inches long. They may be lifted in the autumn and stored like celery in a coldframe or a cellar.

ONION

The onion will thrive under a wide variety of climatic and soil conditions. It does best with an abundance of moisture and a temperate climate without extremes of heat or cold during the growing season. In the South the onion will thrive during the fall, winter, and spring. Farther north winter temperatures may be too severe for certain types; yet others, such as the Potato onion, may be planted in the autumn and be ready for use in early spring. However, in the North onions are primarily a spring, summer, and fall crop. Approximate planting dates are given in Tables 1 and 2.

Any type of soil will grow onions, but it must be fertile, moist, and in the highest state of tilth. Both rotted manure and commercial fer-

FIGURE 24.—Leek. This relative of the onion is used in soups and stews and in other ways

tilizer, especially one high in phosphorus and potash, should be applied to the onion plot. A pound of manure to each square foot of ground and 4 or 5 pounds of fertilizer to each 100 square feet is about right. The soil should be very fine and free from clods and foreign matter.

Onions may be started in the home garden by the use of sets, seedlings, or seed. Sets, or small onions, grown the previous year, are usually employed by home gardeners, but plants grown in an outdoor seed bed in the South or in a hotbed or a greenhouse are coming into more general use. The home-garden culture of onions from seed is quite satisfactory in the northern tier of States, where the summers are comparatively cool.

Several distinct types of onions may be used in the home garden. The Potato or Multiplier variety is planted in the fall or early spring for green onions. The Top or Tree onion is used in the same way. The Bermuda is a large, flat, mild-flavored type that is used extensively in home gardens for growing green onions and dry bulbs. Unfortunately, it is a poor keeper. The Valencia or Spanish variety and its modified form, the Prizetaker, is a large, mild-flavored, straw-colored, spherical onion that is a good keeper. The White Globe, American Silverskin, or White Portugal, and the Yellow Danvers, Southport Yellow Globe, and Southport Red Globe are varieties commonly used as sets and seed for the main or northern crop. All of them may be used for either green or dry onions.

FIGURE 25.—A bunch of onion plants which when planted in the garden yielded over a bushel of good onions

Onion sets, seedlings, or seed may be planted in rows, as suggested in Table 3. The cost of sets and seedlings is about the same, but seed costs much less. In certainty of results the seedlings are best; practically none form seed stalks, and all make onions. Figure 25 shows a bunch of Prizetaker seedlings. This bunch yielded over a bushel of good onions. Seed-sown onions are uncertain unless conditions are quite favorable.

The cultivation of onions may be limited to the control of weeds. When the bulbs are well grown and the tops begin to die, the onions should be pulled and left in windrows in the garden or on wire-bottom trays placed under an open shed for a few days to dry. The tops may then be removed and the onions put in a well-ventilated place to cure.

### SHALLOT

The shallot is a small onion of the Multiplier type. In its requirements it is similar to other onions; and as the bulbs have a more delicate flavor than most onions, the plant is well worth attention in the garden. Shallots seldom form seed and are propagated by means of the small cloves or divisions into which the plant splits during growth. The plant is hardy and may be left in the ground from year to year, but best results are to be had by lifting the clusters of bulbs at the end of the growing season and replanting the smaller ones at the desired time. The Jersey or False shallot is the only kind available from American seedmen. Its quality is much the same as that of the True shallot.

### FLESHY-FRUITED WARM-SEASON CROPS

Eggplant, peppers, and tomatoes are closely related and are similar in their cultural requirements. Warm weather and fertile, well-drained soil are essential to obtaining good results with these crops. Tomatoes are by far the most important, and a home garden without them is rarely seen. Tomatoes are one of the best sources of vitamins A, B, and C. Moreover, the fact that the canned and dried tomatoes also contain these vitamins gives the vegetable added value.

### EGGPLANT

Eggplant is extremely sensitive to the conditions under which it is grown. Distinctly a warm-weather plant, it demands a growing season of from 100 to 140 days with high average day and night temperatures. The soil, also, must be well warmed up before eggplant can safely be set outdoors.

In the South, eggplants may be grown during the spring and autumn; both midsummer and winter conditions are too severe. In the North, summer culture alone is practiced. The more northerly locations, where a short growing season and low summer temperatures prevail, are unsuitable for eggplants. Tables 1 and 2 give the approximate planting dates.

Soil for the eggplant must be extremely fertile, but it is not wise to use fresh manure or large quantities of commercial fertilizer. Garden soil that is very fertile as the result of long-continued good treatment is best for eggplant. Under such conditions a few plants will yield a large number of fruits.

Eggplant seed should be sown in the hotbed, in the greenhouse, or in warm sections outdoors about eight weeks before the plants are needed. It is important that they be kept growing without check from drying, low temperature, or other cause. They may be transplanted like tomatoes. Good plants have stems that are not hard or woody; one with a woody stem rarely develops satisfactorily. Black Beauty and Florida Highbush are good varieties.

### PEPPERS

Peppers have greatly increased in popularity as a home-garden crop. Formerly looked upon as of merit mainly for seasoning, they are now used in salads, pickles, as cooked vegetables, and in many other ways.

Peppers are much like tomatoes in their requirements, but are more exacting. They may be grown over a wide portion of the

United States, in locations where fertile soil and ample moisture with a relatively long growing season of high temperature are found. Being hot-weather plants, peppers can not be planted in the North until the soil has warmed up and all danger of frost has passed. In the South planting dates vary according to the location, fall planting being practiced in some locations. Planting dates are given in Tables 1 and 2.

Plants of peppers should be started six to eight weeks before needed. The seeds and plants require a somewhat higher temperature than those of the tomato. Otherwise they are handled in exactly the same way. In the garden, peppers should be planted in rows as specified in Table 3. They need only sufficient cultivation to keep down weeds.

Varieties of peppers vary widely in their characteristics. Hot peppers, such as are used for flavoring and sauces, are represented by varieties like Small Chili and Long Red. For stuffing or for pickles, the mild-flavored Chinese Giant, Bull Nose, Sweet Mountain, and Harris Early Giant are good sorts. For slicing like tomatoes and cucumbers, Sunnybrook (fig. 26) and Red Squash are recommended.[19]

FIGURE 26.—Sunnybrook peppers, a salad variety

### TOMATO

The tomato is easily entitled to a place among the half-dozen most important home garden vegetables. It grows under a wide variety of conditions, requires but small space for a large production, and its value in the diet is hard to overestimate. It is one of the richest sources of vitamins A, B, and C. Of tropical American origin, the tomato naturally requires a rather high temperature. Home gardens in the extreme South, however, may include tomatoes during the winter. Over most of the upper South and the North it is suited to spring, summer, and autumn culture. In the more northern regions the growing season is liable to be too short for obtaining heavy yields, and in much of the North it is desirable to increase earliness and the length of the growing season by starting the plants indoors. By adopting a few precautions, the home gardener may grow tomatoes in practically all locations where there is fertile soil with sufficient moisture.

---

[19] For additional information on this vegetable see the mimeographed circular obtainable from the Division of Horticultural Crops and Diseases, Bureau of Plant Industry, U. S. Department of Agriculture.

Tomatoes may be grown on any fertile, well-drained garden soil. A liberal application of manure and commercial fertilizer in preparing the soil should be sufficient for tomatoes under most conditions. In applying manure or fertilizer it is well to avoid the excessive use of such materials as poultry manure and fertilizers having a heavy proportion of nitrogen, as these might give too much vine growth and cause failure to set fruits. Heavy applications of manure and fertilizer should be broadcast, not applied in the row; but small quantities may be mixed with the soil in the row in preparing for planting.

Tomato plants should be started from five to seven weeks before they are needed. Enough plants for the home garden may be started in a window box and transplanted to small pots, paper drinking cups, with the bottoms removed, so-called plant bands, which are round or square, or other boxes of soil, the seedlings being spaced 2 or 3 inches apart. Tomato seed germinates best at about 70° F., or ordinary house temperature. After transplanting, tomato plants should be grown at rather low temperatures with plenty of ventilation, as in a coldframe. This gives stocky, hardy growth. If desired tomato plants may be transplanted again to larger containers, such as 4-inch clay pots or quart cans with holes in the bottom.

Tomato plants for all but the early spring crop are usually grown in outdoor seed beds without transplanting. Thin seeding and careful weed control will give strong, stocky plants.

For early tomatoes Earliana, Bonny Best, and Break O'Day varieties are recommended. For medium and late plantings Marglobe, Globe, Greater Baltimore, and Stone are recommended. Stone is distinctly a late variety.

Tomatoes are sensitive to cold and should not be planted until danger of frost is past. By using plant protectors during cold periods the home gardener can set tomato plants somewhat earlier than would otherwise be possible. Hot, dry weather, such as occurs in midsummer in the South, is also unfavorable for planting tomatoes. Fall plantings must be made in accordance with the location. Approximate planting dates are given in Tables 1 and 2. Planting distances depend on the variety and whether the plants are to be pruned and staked or not. If pruned to one stem, trained and tied to stakes or a trellis, they may be set 18 inches apart in 3-foot rows; if not, they may be planted 3 feet apart in 4-foot rows. Pruning and staking has many advantages for the home gardener. Cultivation is easier, a greater yield may be obtained from the same area, and the fruits are always clean and easy to find.[20]

### MISCELLANEOUS VEGETABLES

Florence fennel, martynia, physalis, okra, and sweet corn are grouped together because they can not be conveniently classified elsewhere.

#### FLORENCE FENNEL

Florence fennel is related to celery and celeriac, the enlarged, flattened leaf stalks being the portion used. For a summer crop the seeds are sown in the rows in spring, and for an autumn and winter

---

[20] For additional information on tomato culture, insects, and diseases, see Farmers' Bulletins No. 1233, Tomatoes for Canning and Manufacturing; No. 1338, Tomatoes as a Truck Crop; No. 1371, Diseases and Insects of Garden Vegetables.

crop in the South they are sown toward the end of summer. The plants should be thinned to stand about 6 inches apart. Like most vegetables, fennel needs a fertile soil and an abundance of moisture. When the leaf stalks have grown to about 2 inches in diameter the plants may be slightly mounded up and partially blanched. They should be harvested and used before they become tough and stringy. Fennel is cooked and used like celeriac and kohlrabi.

### MARTYNIA

Martynia requires a good deal of heat and therefore is grown only during the warmer portion of the season. The excessive heat of southern midsummer, however, especially when accompanied by drought, is not favorable to the crop; neither is low temperature. Its growing conditions are very similar to those of cucumbers and squashes. The seeds may be started indoors and transplanted to the garden, or they may be drilled in the rows where the crop is to be grown. Planting dates and spacing are given in Tables 1, 2, and 3. The fruits, gathered while young and tender, are used for pickles.

### OKRA

Okra, or gumbo, has about the same degree of hardiness as cucumbers and tomatoes and may be grown under conditions suitable for them. It will thrive on any fertile, well-drained soil. An abundance of quickly available plant food will stimulate growth and insure a good yield of tender, high-quality pods.

As okra is a warm-weather vegetable, the seeds should not be sown until the soil is warm. Planting dates are given in Table 1. The rows should be from 3 to 5 feet apart, depending on whether the variety is a dwarf or large growing. Seeds should be sown every few inches and the plants thinned to stand 18 inches to 2 feet apart in the rows. Perkins, Mammoth, Dwarf Green Prolific, White Velvet, and Lady Finger are good varieties. The pods should all be picked young and tender, and none allowed to ripen. Old pods are unfit for use and soon exhaust the plant.[21]

### PHYSALIS

Physalis, also known as ground cherry and husk tomato, is closely related to the tomato and can be grown in any location where tomatoes do well. The kind ordinarily grown in gardens produces a yellow fruit about the size of a cherry. The seeds may be started indoors or sown in the rows in the garden. Planting dates and spacing are given in Tables 1, 2, and 3. The fruits are used for making preserves.

### SWEET CORN

Sweet corn, like potatoes and sweetpotatoes, requires considerable space and is adapted only to large gardens. Although a warm-weather plant, it may be grown in practically all parts of the United States. It requires a fertile, well-drained, but moist soil. With these requirements met, the type of the soil does not seem to be especially important, but a clay loam is almost ideal for sweet corn.

---

[21] For additional information see Farmers' Bulletin 232, Okra: Its Culture and Uses.

In the South sweet corn is planted from early spring until autumn, but the corn earworm, drought, and heat make it difficult to obtain worth-while results in midsummer. The ears pass the edible stage very quickly, and succession plantings should be made to insure a constant supply. In the North sweet corn can not be safely planted until the ground has thoroughly warmed up. Here, too, succession plantings need to be made to insure a steady supply. Planting dates are given in Tables 1 and 2. Sweet corn is frequently planted to good advantage after early potatoes, peas, beets, lettuce, or some other early, short-season crop. In some cases, to gain time, it may be planted before the early crop is removed.

Sweet corn may be grown in either hills or drills in rows at least 3 feet apart. It is well to plant the seed rather thickly and thin to single stocks 12 to 15 inches apart, or three or four plants to each 3-foot hill. For early corn Golden Bantam, Early Minnesota, and Adams Early are suggested. Early Evergreen, Evergreen, and Country Gentleman are recommended for later planting.

Experiments have shown that in the eastern part of the country there is no advantage in removing suckers from sweet corn. Cultivation sufficient to control weeds is all that is needed.

# ORGANIZATION OF THE UNITED STATES DEPARTMENT OF AGRICULTURE WHEN THIS PUBLICATION WAS LAST PRINTED

| | |
|---|---|
| *Secretary of Agriculture* | ARTHUR M. HYDE. |
| *Assistant Secretary* | R. W. DUNLAP. |
| *Director of Scientific Work* | A. F. WOODS. |
| *Director of Regulatory Work* | W. G. CAMPBELL. |
| *Director of Extension Work* | C. W. WARBURTON. |
| *Director of Personnel and Business Administration.* | W. W. STOCKBERGER. |
| *Director of Information* | M. S. EISENHOWER. |
| *Solicitor* | E. L. MARSHALL. |
| *Weather Bureau* | CHARLES F. MARVIN, *Chief.* |
| *Bureau of Animal Industry* | JOHN R. MOHLER, *Chief.* |
| *Bureau of Dairy Industry* | O. E. REED, *Chief.* |
| *Bureau of Plant Industry* | WILLIAM A. TAYLOR, *Chief.* |
| *Forest Service* | R. Y. STUART, *Chief.* |
| *Bureau of Chemistry and Soils* | H. G. KNIGHT, *Chief.* |
| *Bureau of Entomology* | C. L. MARLATT, *Chief.* |
| *Bureau of Biological Survey* | PAUL G. REDINGTON, *Chief.* |
| *Bureau of Public Roads* | THOMAS H. MACDONALD, *Chief.* |
| *Bureau of Agricultural Engineering* | S. H. MCCRORY, *Chief.* |
| *Bureau of Agricultural Economics* | NILS A. OLSEN, *Chief.* |
| *Bureau of Home Economics* | LOUISE STANLEY, *Chief.* |
| *Plant Quarantine and Control Administration* | LEE A. STRONG, *Chief.* |
| *Grain Futures Administration* | J. W. T. DUVEL, *Chief.* |
| *Food and Drug Administration* | WALTER G. CAMPBELL, *Director of Regulatory Work, in Charge.* |
| *Office of Experiment Stations* | J. T. JARDINE, *Chief.* |
| *Office of Cooperative Extension Work* | C. B. SMITH, *Chief.* |
| *Library* | CLARIBEL R. BARNETT, *Librarian.* |

For sale by the Superintendent of Documents, Washington, D. C. - - - - - - Price 10 cents